SACRED and PROFANE LOVE

TWO PLAYS BY EDMOND ROSTAND

Creator of *Cyrano de Bergerac*

Genge Press

Earlier publications by Genge Press relating to Edmond Rostand:

THE MAN WHO WAS CYRANO – A LIFE OF EDMOND ROSTAND, CREATOR OF *CYRANO DE BERGERAC*, by Sue Lloyd, with notes, index, bibliography and appendix (USA, UP, 2003; UK, Genge Press, 2007) The first and only biography in English of the French dramatist.

THE TWO PIERROTS or THE WHITE SUPPER (*Les Deux Pierrots ou Le Souper Blanc*) (Genge Press, 2007). A new verse translation by Thom Christoph of Rostand's witty early curtain-raiser, with an introduction by Sue Lloyd. This three-hander has been a favourite with amateurs and already reveals Rostand's dramatic talents.

CHANTECLER, by Edmond Rostand: (Genge Press, 2010) the original French text with English introduction, comprehensive notes and chronology by Sue Lloyd. Written with Rostand's characteristic verve and humour, *Chantecler* also contains some of his most lyrical writing, including the famous 'Hymn to the Sun'.

Updates of work in progress, and bibliographies of the works of Edmond Rostand and of the English verse dramatist, Christopher Fry, may be found on our new website gengepress.blogspot.com (formerly www.gengepress.co.uk).

SACRED and PROFANE LOVE
TWO PLAYS BY EDMOND ROSTAND:

The Woman of Samaria *(La Samaritaine)*

English version by Philippa Gerry & Sue Lloyd

The Last Night of Don Juan *(La Dernière Nuit de Don Juan)*

English version by Sonia Yates & Sue Lloyd

Genge Press

Genge Press, 45 Quay St., Minehead, TA24 5UL

gengepress@aol.com; gengepress.blogspot.com

ISBN 978-0-9549043-6-4

A CIP record for this book is available from the British
Cataloguing in Publication data office

For performance rights please contact gengepress@aol.com

Printed by First Design Print Web, Porlock

PREFACE

All his life, Edmond Rostand strove to inspire his audiences with his own idealistic and enthusiastic attitude to life. In *Cyrano de Bergerac* in particular, he succeeded. But all his plays are worth reading and all share the same passion for positive action, creativity and love. Love can mean many things. For Rostand's heroes, true love means selflessness, faithfulness, purity and truth. Play after play demonstrates the power of such love to transform and redeem the lives of the hero and other characters. This 'sacred' love is contrasted with the kind of physical love which is inspired by selfish sensual desire: 'profane' love.

Here are new translations of two contrasting Rostand plays, one an early play describing the positive power of 'sacred' love, the other, written much later, showing how 'profane' love can destroy a human soul. In *La Samaritaine*, a story taken from St John's Gospel in the New Testament, the love of God as mediated through Jesus Christ is reciprocated by Christ's hearers and transforms the life of a woman who until then has only experienced 'profane' love.

Using a more negative approach in his version of the Don Juan legend in *La Dernière Nuit de Don Juan*, Rostand illustrates the destructiveness of purely selfish 'profane' love. Here the Don's egotistic arrogance and licentiousness is contrasted with the 'sacred' love of a woman he once seduced, who tries to save him from both himself and eternal damnation.

Edmond Rostand once said that in his dramas he is offering us 'leçons d'âme' (lessons for the soul). These plays present two opposed ways of looking at sacred and profane love, but with the same lessons for the soul.

Both these translations are, sadly, in prose. For the full beauty of Rostand's verse, we urge you to read them also in the original French.

SML, Minehead, 2015

The Woman of Samaria (La Samaritaine)

Edmond Rostand

A play in three tableaux

English version by Philippa Gerry
& Sue Lloyd

INTRODUCTION TO *THE WOMAN OF SAMARIA*

Edmond Rostand's plays live on because they express something eternal in the human spirit: idealism. Rostand's idealism was not a reasoned philosophy but rather an emotional response which set spiritual values against materialistic ones, and sincerity against cynicism. For him, it is the spiritual dimension that makes life worth living, raising the ordinary to the sublime. It was his avowed aim to write plays to inspire his compatriots with sincerity and passion.

All Rostand's plays contain what he called 'lessons for the soul'. The theme of *La Samaritaine* is the power of God's love to transform our lives. Although Jesus's divinity is made clear, it is his teaching rather than his role as a Saviour which is central to this play. Rostand, whose Catholic mother had ensured he was educated at a Catholic college, was familiar with bible stories such as this one. But he was not a practising Catholic as an adult and in his work preferred to stress the spiritual aspects of Christianity rather than Christ as Redeemer on the cross.

When and why the play was written

La Samaritaine was written in 1897 for the celebrated actress Sarah Bernhardt and first performed in Paris on 14th April that year. Edmond Rostand was just twenty-nine years old, but he was already displaying the talent for the theatre that ten months later would make him famous world-wide with the amazing success of *Cyrano de Bergerac*.

Rostand's stage career had begun in 1894, when *Les Romanesques*, a play in verse, like all his plays, had been well-received at the Comédie-Française. Sarah, now in her fifties, was looking for poetical works of just the kind Rostand wanted to write, and agreed to put on Rostand's *La Princesse lointaine* in 1895. This dreamy and poetic play pleased the first-night audience but not the critics, and closed earlier than planned. But Sarah had faith in Rostand's talent and commissioned another play, this time with a religious theme, as it was to be performed at Easter.

When reading Ernest Renan's *Vie de Jesus* (published in 1863) some years earlier, Rostand had felt that Jesus's conversion of the woman of Samaria would make a good play. And the role of courtesan would not be a new one for Sarah, famous for her role as 'La Dame aux Camélias' in the younger Dumas's eponymous play.

Rostand gave the woman the name Photine but otherwise kept closely to the story as told in St John's Gospel (John IV, 1-42). In order to make Sarah's role of the Samaritan woman the central character, he had to invent a whole second act showing how she returns to the town and persuades the people there to come and see Jesus. But all Jesus's teaching in the play is taken from the gospels.

In choosing the Samaritan woman as his heroine, Rostand may also have been recalling images from his childhood. In the church at Bagnères de Luchon, a spa in the Hautes Pyrénées, where he spent his summer holidays as a child and youth until 1895, were a tapestry and a fresco on this very subject, which was also depicted in a mural at the town's thermal baths.

In the story as told by St John, Jesus redeems Photine by speaking to her about the living water that is the love of God. Again, memories of Luchon may have been an influence on Rostand's choice of subject, for in a long poem written in 1893, 'L'Eau', he credits Luchon with inspiring his love of flowing water; this poem includes the thought that Luchon has enough fountains for any number of Samaritan women.

Both *La Princesse lointaine* and *La Samaritaine* are idealistic, poetic plays in verse, but public and critics alike warmed more to *La Samaritaine*, perhaps because it was a familiar story. Sarah lavished money on the costumes and scenery, and the première, this time, was a great success. Sarah continued to revive the play, especially at Easter, at home and abroad, and chose to record some of Photine's speeches for her first gramophone recording. *La Samaritaine* remained a favourite with the public and with those of Rostand's poetic contemporaries who later felt that the poet had lost his way in writing a heroic comedy, *Cyrano de Bergerac*. English poets such as Christopher Fry also loved this play.

La Samaritaine has been translated into English rhymed verse by Mrs Henderson Dangerfield Norman as *The Woman of Samaria* (Collected Plays of Edmond Rostand, vol. 1 (New York & London: Macmillan, 1921; republished by Bibibliolife LLC, 2011)). There is also a modern annotated French edition by Philippe Bulinge (L'Harmattan, 2004). An English version by Wilfred Grantham and May Agate, *The Woman of Samaria*, with music by Maurice Jacobson, was broadcast by the BBC in July 1945. The play has been translated into several languages including German, Italian, Hungarian and Polish.

The aim of this prose version has been to convey as much as possible of the beauty of Rostand's verse in the lyrical passages, while using a modern idiom in the more conversational scenes. We have indented songs and lyrical passages, as in the original text. Where touches of local colour explain themselves, they have been left; others have been paraphrased. The former town of Sichem ('Sychar' in the Authorized Version) was also known as 'Shechem'. We have kept Rostand's usage for this and other place names.

The Action of the Play

La Samaritaine is described by Rostand as an 'Évangile en trois tableaux'. The only act with much dramatic tension is the second act, although there are several *coups de théâtre*, so the term 'tableaux' suggests that the pleasure given by the play will be visual as well as aural.

Rostand sets the scene in a dramatic Prologue, with the stage in semi-darkness. Three phantoms are speaking beside Jacob's Well in Samaria. They are Abraham, Isaac and Jacob, drawn by a mysterious force to celebrate the arrival of the Messiah at the well Jacob himself had dug. As they fade away with the coming of the dawn, the living take their place. The Samaritans from the nearby town of Sichem meet here to bewail their oppression by the Romans and the contemptuous dismissal of their religion by the Jews, who treat them as heretics because they worship God on nearby Mount Garizim and not in Jerusalem.

The Samaritan people hope for the Messiah to come and save them, but when Jesus and his disciples appear, they are not recognised but spurned as Jews. The disciples go into the local town to buy food, leaving Jesus alone by the well. Rostand, like Renan and Victor Hugo in *La Fin de Satan*, portrays Jesus as a gentle, softly-spoken young man, attractive in character and in looks, the 'beloved of souls' (Hugo). Jesus is beautiful and eloquent because God's love shines through him.

Photine, who has come from Sichem to draw water at the well, appears with her water jar. At first she ignores Jesus, but when he starts talking to her about living water, her interest is aroused. On learning that Jesus is the Messiah who was to come, she instinctively worships him by singing the love song based on the *Song of Solomon* that she had been singing earlier. She is ashamed, but Jesus tells her that human love is a preparation for loving God. The tableau ends with Photine sitting at Jesus's feeet, listening attentively as he preaches the gospel of love to her. Her repeated phrase 'I am listening' hangs in the air as the curtain falls.

The Second Tableau opens in contrast on the bustling, worldly day-to-day life of Sichem. The disciples are trying in vain to buy food from the hostile Samaritans in the busy market-place. They leave almost empty-handed in a hail of insults. Soon after, Photine bursts on stage, full of her good news that the Messiah has come. At first treated with scorn as a well-known courtesan, she eventually persuades some of the people to follow her back to Jesus. The priest arrives and is amazed when the illiterate Photine argues with him in the words of the Old Testament. The priest insists on the old order, 'la loi' (the law), while Photine is preaching the new order 'la foi' (faith), brought by Jesus.

As the subversive nature of Jesus's teaching becomes clear, the priest sends someone for the Romans. Meanwhile Photine's eloquence is winning over the crowd. In a long, lyrical speeech, she tells the people that Jesus's teaching can be expressed in one word, 'Love'.

When the Roman soldiers arrive, Photine is accused of announcing the arrival of the Messiah who will set the Jews free from Roman rule. She is seized and bound. But just as it seems her mission will fail, the centurion in charge of the soldiers learns that she has been speaking about Jesus. The centurion, who recalls that Jesus said 'Render unto Caesar what is Caesar's', considers him a poor simple Jew who is no threat to Roman rule. He immediately sets Photine free and marches his soldiers away.

Photine has to explain to the now reluctant townsfolk that Jesus's kingdom is not of this world. And for various reasons: hope, curiosity, ambition, faith, they all agree to come and see this Messiah. The act concludes dramatically with the townspeople, led by a victorious Photine, streaming out of the town gate singing a psalm of praise.

For the Third Tableau we return to Jacob's Well. The disciples are grumbling about Jesus's choice of Photine, the lowest of the low, to take his message to the town. Jesus is sitting a little way off. He senses the approach of the townspeople before they appear, garlanded and waving palms, and singing joyfully. The excitement of the crowd as it reaches the Messiah is calmed immediately when Jesus speaks. He preaches to them about love, and tells them God is spirit, to be worshipped everywhere, not in any particular temple. He heals the sick in body and mind and agrees to stay with them for two days. The Tableau closes reverently and peacefully with Photine kneeling before Jesus, repeating the prayer he has taught her, 'Our Father ...' On the crowd's reverent 'Amen', the curtain falls.

Apparently even the cast found this act so moving that it brought tears to their eyes at every performance. Rostand's lyrical verse, enhanced by Gabriel Pierné's music; Sarah's presence and thrilling voice; the attractive costumes and decor, and the impressive tableaux, must have combined to make the play an almost mystical experience, as many have testified.

Rostand's Attitude to Life and Religion

In *La Samaritaine,* Rostand stresses three aspects of Jesus's teaching: the spiritual nature of true worship; the power of God's love to inspire and redeem, and respect for all human beings, however humble or despised.

Rostand is faithful to the message in St John's Gospel: God is to be worshipped in spirit and in truth. Photine and her compatriots are assured that God can be worshipped anywhere, not just in a particular temple. This problem had led to enmity between Jews and Samaritans, with the result that many, such as Photine, did not worship God at all.

Rostand himself had little patience with rites and dogma. 'L'important, c'est qu'un coeur nous batte dans la torse' says Frère Trophime, the good priest in *La Princesse lointaine* ('The important thing is that we have a heart beating inside us'). Rostand's Cyrano de Bergerac is portrayed as caring little for the duties of an orthodox Catholic, yet the Mother Superior says of him : 'Dieu doit bien le connaître' (God certainly knows him).

The redeming power of love is the main theme of this play, as it had been of *La Princesse lointaine.* In the earlier play, it is the ideal love of the troubadour Joffroy Rudel for his 'distant princess' Mélissinde, that leads the princess and the other characters to the love of God. In *La Samaritaine,* the sensual love of a courtesan is converted by Jesus into the spiritual love of God.

Respect and sympathy for all beings, especially the humblest or most despised, is a constant theme in Rostand's writing from his earliest poems, published as *Les Musardises* in 1890. These were dedicated to 'Les Ratés', those who failed because they aimed too high. In *La Samaritaine,* Jesus's choice of Photine, held in low esteem by the townsfolk, who disapproved of her behaviour, was criticised by the disciples, but she won over the town for him. 'Always the lowliest', Jesus murmurs to himself when Photine confesses her belief that a Messiah should come, 'Thank you, my Father'.

Rostand stresses that Jesus's message is an inclusive one: he is the shepherd of all peoples, regardless of their beliefs and forms of worship. In his last great play, *Chantecler*, the creator is named as 'Le Berger'. In *La Samaritaine*, Rostand was expressing his own sincere, if unorthodox, religious feeling, which, portrayed in the most artistic way and the most reverently lyrical verse of which he was capable, struck a corresponding chord in his audience. The translators believe that modern audiences, too, will respond to this gentle and moving play, which is as relevant today as when it was first performed.

TABLEAU ONE

Le Puits de Jacob

Jacob's Well is situated at the intersection of the two great roads which lead, one to Mesopotamia, the other towards the Great Sea, not far from the former town of Sichem, in Samaria.

It is a vast oblong tank, with a low rim on which people can sit. A half-ruined stone vault still arches above this well. The rope which raises or lowers the water jugs is worked by a rough-hewn wooden handle.

An enormous wild fig tree stretches out its branches horizontally. Beside it is one of those olive trees whose pale leaves are more silvery in Samaria than elsewhere. Further away are several terebinth trees and the svelte silhouettes of cypresses.

In the background is a dusty green embankment where the white roads meet; from it a winding path leads down to the well. Behind the embankment, the blue valley of Sichem is visible.

Mount Ebal and Mount Garizim edge the horizon. On Garizim a ruined temple is etched against the sky; in the hollow between the two hills, the pale, square houses of Sichem are dotted about.

This is how the scene will look in daylight. But as the curtain rises, it is still dark, a beautiful transparent darkness, bright with stars showing. Standing on the stones beside the well, in the deeper blackness of the vault, is a very tall white phantom with a centenarian's beard, leaning on a shepherd's staff. A second phantom just as tall and just as white, stands motionless on one of the steps. A third, like the first two, with the same beard, the same staff, is advancing mysteriously towards them. The third is the first to speak.

Scene One

THE PHANTOMS

First Phantom [Isaac], *gliding towards the well.*

Floating on the night breeze, and free to roam until dawn, I come without knowing why, just as I am, a phantom. I come on silent sandalled feet, gliding back and forth ... But O, adored Jehovah! Who is that other tall phantom standing close to the well?

Second Phantom [Abraham], *to the first.*

White bearded shape in the dark night, were you once alive? Have you emerged from Sheol, where they sleep in flowerless meadows and walk under a moonless sky? Are you a spirit?

First Phantom [Isaac]

I am.

Second Phantom [Abraham]

I recognise your voice, my son.

First Phantom [Isaac]

But there is another phantom standing on the step, clothed in white ...

To the third phantom.

Motionless phantom, do you hear me?

Third Phantom [Jacob]

I recognise your voice, father.

Second Phantom [Abraham]

It is the child more pious than Job, standing there on the step.

Third Phantom [Jacob]

Father!

First Phantom [Isaac]

The Patriarch!

Third Phantom

Abraham!

Second Phantom [Abraham]

Isaac!

First Phantom [Isaac]

Jacob!

Jacob

What holy summons has roused us to walk again on the sweet, firm earth?

Isaac

There must be some momentous reason why the green-winged dark angel left the pale gates of Sheol ajar this evening.

Jacob, *to Abraham.*

What hopes are springing to birth? Tell us, do, what startled our shades and brought us out this evening? You must know what is to come, you whose hundred and seventy years have brought you closer to Jehovah.

Abraham, *to Isaac.*

Why are you kissing this dusty road so reverently?

Isaac

I feel bound to do this by some obscure presentiment.

Abraham, *to Jacob.*

Why are you kissing the rim of the well that you dug here?

Jacob

Some supernatural force is calling me to worship it — and you, why do you breathe in this silent air so tenderly?

Abraham

I am kissing in this air, before it comes, the Voice which will make it vibrate!

Isaac

A voice, Patriarch?

Abraham

He is coming, he is coming, he is on his way! You can be sure of it, for as I passed Moses as he lay in his bed in desolate Sheol tonight, he whispered it to me, putting his finger to his lips.

Jacob, *prostrating himself with Isaac.*

Our hearts are softly singing psalms.

Abraham

Long before the blue of night falls again on roofs of golden thatch, there will be sighs sweeter than balm, words greater than kingdoms ... That is why our three ghosts have come wandering to this well.

Jacob, *to Isaac.*

Can it be possible, Father, that of all the wells on earth, the Lord has chosen, for I know not what great mystery, the well I dug with my own hands?

Isaac

My son, you can be proud! You were the worker he chose to dig the well of salvation whose water will revive the wan-faced future; this is so fine a thought that the honour of being your father or your ancestor makes us feel that our winding sheets have become cloaks of glory!

Now the stage fills with phantoms.

Jacob

But look! Here are all those who came to draw water from this well, long after I ceased to do so ... First one and then another, and now a long wavering file of phantoms, slowly winding here in holy gladness to kiss this grey well-rim. All the Underworld is astir; I can see Joseph and Joshua.

Abraham

Phantoms pouring along the paths, come and fall on your knees at the Well of love!

A glimmer of light shows in the east.

But look! Already daylight is gilding the town and its tower ... our shapes will soon dissolve.

Jacob

And soon, of the three phantoms that were here, only three shrinking pale shapes will remain, three long waving beards that become three small silvery wisps, melting away like mist.

Isaac

A crowd is approaching in the distance. It is the Samaritans, who come here secretly early in the morning, to share their fears with each other.

Abraham

These are the men of Sichem, who come full of their grievances, to talk beneath the terebinth trees about their undying hatred of Rome and Jerusalem.

Jacob

Let us vanish at their approach. ...

And you, dreaming witnesses that surround us — earth that holds such tender recollections; sky with your wise stars; hills where every rock keeps a memory of the Past, and you too, well dug by my own spade — you have just heard how the dead are waiting expectantly for the approaching feet of a second, more gentle, Moses. Now you will hear how the living await His coming.

Scene Two

THE PRIEST, AZRIEL, YOUNG PEOPLE, OLD FOLK, TRADERS ETC.
They come on stage at a slow and mournful pace and stop in front of the well. They begin to lament together.

A Man

This is the well, with its rim and its steps, that was dug in this field by Jacob, the most holy patriarch, son of Isaac who was son of Abraham. He was wise in the ways of heaven.

A Second Man

The sorrows of Leah are still here among the flowers.

A Third Man

This dust once adored the shadows of your gestures, Rachel.

A Fourth Man

On the slopes of this mountain those who carried the holy Ark set it down while they paused for breath.

A Fifth Man

On the day when Abraham held nothing back from God, the ram was caught by its horns in this very bush.

A Sixth Man

This lingering perfume, borne on the breeze, comes from incense in the tomb of Joseph.

An Old Man

On this ground, Joshua set up the twelve stone slabs.

A Second Old Man

This air is made of immortal breaths.

A Young Man

Here, a glory gilds the light ...

The Priest

And that is why it seemed to me a good place, chief men of Sichem and men of Samaria, to hold a discussion about the evils afflicting our land.

A Man, *turning to face the ruins on Mount Garizim. All turn like him and prostrate themselves.*

Temple of Garizim, your destruction made the temple of Zion tremble with joy. Even now, the Jews hate your ruins.

A Second Man

The Jews consider us to be a heretical sect.

A Third Man

They say we combine our worship of the true God with false foreign idols with wild and grotesque names like Soukkoth-Bénoth, or Thartaq!

A Fourth Man

Or Zéboub, god of the flies!

First Old Man

It is all lies! We are the only ones who preserve the true Jewish faith.

Second Old Man

Yes! We alone keep the original texts, the Pentateuch, enclosed in a copper casket.

The Priest

This Book was copied out on a sheepskin, with the utmost care, on the threshold of the Tabernacle, by Abischouah …

First Old Man

Who was descended from Eléazar, the son of Aaron …

Second Old Man

                                        Who was Moses' brother.

A Young Man

So why is it we, who keep the true faith, who are despised?

A Second Young Man

We are greeted with disgust, like scorpions coming out of a basilica.

The Priest

We only have a hovel in which to worship.

First Old Man

The Romans oppress us and the Jews insult us.

A Man

A Pharisee who strictly obeys his laws has to wash his hands if he so much as plucks a jasmine branch from beside our footpaths.

A Second Man

And if he sits under one of our trees, he has to wash off its shadow three times with purified water.

A Young Man

It's too much to bear!

Another Young Man

And even while we suffer these insults from the Jews, the eagle's wing of the Romans beats us about the head!

Another Young Man

It's too much to bear. Let's revolt!

A Man

No! Let's just look after our vineyards.

First Old Man, *to the man who has just spoken.*

So you are resigned to living with our shame?

The Man

But ...

First Old Man

Doesn't your soul sometimes rise up in disgust?

The Man

I try to forget our sorrows.

First Old Man

So you turn to drink.

The Man

Well, why else are the slopes of Mount Ebal covered with wreathed vines? I'm trying to forget. I'm just doing what Noah did. The heathens have taught me to love Bacchus.

Azriel, *who until now has remained silent and listless.*

He's right. It's an impossible struggle.

First Old Man

Yes, of course it's a struggle. It's far more pleasant to lie there without making an effort, wrapped in soft, perfumed arms. You, son, who used to get so angry about these insults once, you now chase after Photine, even though you are her sixth lover. She's already had five before you.

Azriel

I love her. And besides, I don't know where to turn any more. I think it's impossible for us to regain our rights. If an honest man comes along, I am ready to follow him. Meanwhile (*indicating the drunkard*), I do as he does. A light wine helps him to forget. For me, it's the stronger wine of eyes and lips.

First Old Man

It's always the same when we get together: No one has anything to suggest.

A Trader

Yes! I do! I suggest we flatter the Romans, win them over gradually. Then we'll see what can be done about the Jews.

A Man, *bursting violently out of the crowd.*

You! You fear disorder because it is bad for business. The brutal order of the Romans suits you well. You love the sharp-edged sword, and as long as its cutting edge guards your gold, you willingly bear the flat of it across your shoulders, trader!

The Trader

But ...

The Man

Be quiet! Now, as for me, I think we should act at once! Let's revolt! Let's copy Judas the Gaulonite and stop paying taxes, and the tithes on salt, aniseed and cumin!

The Priest

That's right! Steal and destroy, profit from the uproar that would result! That's quite enough. We know you and your dogs of war! Now this is what I propose: let's get together enough money to rebuild the temple — you know it's urgent. The Jews won't be able to prevent this insult to their pride, and their High Priest Caiaphas will die of rage! Our sweet revenge will be to celebrate the feast of Purim on Mount Garizim better than they do. Let's rebuild our temple, friends, let's revive our splendid rituals of worship there — and let's nominate a High Priest, too. Let's hear the blasts from the chiselled silver trumpets soar up again into the starry skies!

The Trader

Now we see the claws beneath the velvet paw! Who is to be the High Priest who will exasperate Caiaphas? You! You would like to wear the ephod of twisted linen thread, the purple robe glittering with golden bells and pomegranates! And you want the people to buy it all for you!

The Priest

Silence, vile trader! Go back to your counter!

The Man who spoke before the trader

The priest is full of venom because we could see into his heart!

The Priest

And haven't I seen into yours, assassin?

The Man

Hypocrite!

The Priest

Thief!

First Old Man, *covering his face with his hands.*

Oh! This is unbearable!

Azriel

Didn't I tell you, there's no hope? Now you see my excuse for inaction: they are all blinded by their own self-interest. It's all over for us. This country is dying.

A Voice from the Crowd

And the Messiah?

Everyone

What? What did he say?

A Shepherd, *stepping forward.*

I said: "And the Messiah?"

The Priest

Yes ... well!

The Shepherd

You speak of him less and less. Is he still coming?

The Priest, *smiling.*

Yes, oh yes.

The Shepherd

>The Christ, as foretold by the prophecy?

The Priest

Yes, yes, of course he will come, the Messiah! We, the priests, will be warned of his coming, and we will let you know about it straight away. (*To the priests around him.*)

>Naive fools! They still hope, even after all this time.

The Shepherd

When will he come?

The Priest

Ah well ... soon, if you pray hard to the Lord and pay for many sacrifices.

The Shepherd

I see. You always say "yes" but you don't actually know anything about it. What will he be like, this Messiah?

A Young Man

>A warrior!

The Priest

>A high priest!

The First Old Man

He will arrive on a cloud!

A Second Young Man

>No! On a hippogriff!

A Third Young Man

There will be two Christs!

A Fourth Young Man

>No, just one!

Various Voices

One! Two! Yes! No!

A Man

But Christ has already come!

Several voices

What is his name, then?

A Young Man

Judas the Gaulonite! ...

Another Young Man

No, you're wrong! John the Baptist!

The Priest

The Christ will be joyful and strong!

An Old Man

No, he will be sad and weak.

A Young Man

He will come if ...

The Trader

No, he will come, but ...

The Shepherd

As he speaks, Jesus appears on the road above the embankment with his disciples.

Ah! I can see that you no longer believe in the Christ, perverse souls, for your belief in him is now only a sham, an excuse for empty arguments. As for me, I tell you that he is coming. Clever minds cannot see clearly any more, now it is the heart which sees. He is coming. What will he be like? Is the trader right, or the priest? I don't know. He will be whatever he wants to be. What right do you have, you who come here just to represent only your own interests, to pour doubts on our hopes, our hopes of ending our sufferings?

I tell you that he is coming! The Samaritans, the real ones, that is, us humble folk, are certain of it. And the force of his anger, like a winnowing wind, will blow away your pride and useless chatter! He is coming, he is there, we can sense it, on the threshold of our times, and we will know how to recognise him without your help.

The Priest

How then?

The Shepherd

I don't know, by his look, perhaps; by the sound of his voice, the gesturing of his hand ...

Jesus, *at the top of the bank, pointing at the distant town.*

Excuse me, is that Sichem?

The Shepherd, *beginning to turn towards him.*

Yes, keep on going!

Scene Three

THE SAME, PLUS JESUS AND HIS DISCIPLES

The Shepherd, *as he sees them.*

Oh, They're Jews! They're Jews!

Everyone, *shouting.*

Heathens! Chase them away!

The Priest

No, treat them with scorn.

The Trader

Let's show our disgust by leaving.

Azriel

Well, I'm staying.

A Young Man

> Why?

Azriel

Photine will come here soon to draw water.

A Second Young Man

Come away with us. Leave them alone.

A Third Young Man

> Let's take him away.

Peter, *to the Samaritans who are leaving.*

What, are you going off without talking to us?

Andrew

> We need food.

A Samaritan

> Eat the brambles, then.

The Drunkard

If you want anything better, you'll have to pay a lot for it. They fleece Jews in Sichem.

Peter, *insolently.*

> You mean Sichar.

An Old Man

Oh my town! This name dishonours you!

A Young Man

Take care! One day we might desecrate your former temple with animal bones.

Peter, *indignant.*

> Oh!

The Priest, *drawing away the young man.*

Let's leave them.

A Samaritan, *turning round as he leaves.*

> Your temple is offensive to God.

They go out.

Peter

You're lying! (*He shouts at their departing backs.*) There's only one temple in the world ...

A Samaritan's distant voice.

> Yes! Ours!

Shouts of laughter.

Scene Four

JESUS AND HIS DISCIPLES

Peter, *coming down the bank.*

A curse on this land! May a plague swallow it up! May swarms of noisy locusts descend on it!

James, *also coming down the bank.*

May blight destroy the fruit on their trees! May their stores be attacked by maggots!

Andrew, *also coming down the bank.*

May their women miscarry and their men be weak! May they know every kind of thirst and hunger! May their enemies surround them and may their cities become desolate ruins!

Peter

And may your fruit trees: lemon, almond, mulberry and pomegranate, never again feel the refreshing dew, or sway and groan under boughs heavy with fruit!

Jesus

The blessings of God upon Samaria!

He too comes down the bank.

Peter

What, Rabbi? But I remember you saying once, 'Go not to the Gentiles and the Samaritans. Only preach to the sheep of Israel'.

Andrew

Yes, you yourself seemed to hate these heathens.

Jesus

I love them.

Peter

But I did hear you say those words, didn't I? Why did you say them?

Jesus

That was in the beginning. Your faith was not yet strong enough to receive all my teaching. If I had told you to love even the Gentiles, you would have been scandalised, my dear children. You were living in the dark. How could I safely shine suddenly into your darkness the full beam of my light? Or all at once pour out for you, weak as you were, all my strong wine? Surely not, and so I was careful at first: I filtered the light, I measured the dose, I did not dare give you everything at once. Now it is time. I do dare.

Andrew

So not being a Jew is not a barrier, then?

Jesus

Elisha cured Naaman and he was a Syrian.

Peter

What! Do you mean we have to love these Samaritans?

Jesus

And you will love them. Because I ask you to.

Peter

What is it you are asking of us, Rabbi?

Jesus

To be perfect. Those who carry my burden, feel their load is lighter. So carry my burden. Love your neighbour.

Peter

So what you call our neighbour can be a base heathen, then?

Jesus

A traveller going to Jericho from Jerusalem fell among thieves. They beat and wounded him and no one heard his cries. They left him for dead. There he lay, just one huge wound, with the blood flowing out of him like wine from a wineskin. A priest came along. He saw this body lying on the blood-soaked ground, and he passed on. Then a levite came along. He saw the light fading in the dim eyes. And he too passed on.

Then a Samaritan came along. He saw the poor wounded head: he jumped off his mule. Hastily he poured on balm mixed with oil to staunch the blood; he gently took the dying man in his arms, and setting him on his saddle, took him to shelter and laid him down on a bed for the night. The next morning at daybreak, he gave the innkeepers two deniers in advance, and said to them, "I am going away. But during my absence, take care of him, dress his wounds. When I return, I will pay for any extra expenses you may incur".

And then this heathen went on his way. Now tell me in all honesty, which of these men behaved like a true neighbour to this poor man abandoned to die like a dog? Was it the priest, the levite or the Samaritan?

Peter

But ...

Jesus

      Have you understood?

James

      We have!

John *to Jesus, leading him to the rim of the well.*

Sit down and rest. It was a long and stony road.

Andrew

And even worse, they say there are terrible robbers down there. There's one especially ... I've forgotten his name ...

Jesus, *softly.*

Barabbas.

John, *kneeling beside him.*

You broke off your story to ask the way. Please go on, we're listening. It was about a man sowing his field.

Jesus, *smiling.*

What do I need to explain?

John

What is the good seed?

Jesus

It is the seed which I sow.

Peter, *sitting down at Jesus's feet.*

And the field?

Jesus

It is the world.

Andrew, *sitting likewise.*

And the harvest?

Jesus

All my chosen ones, the golden grain.

James, *sitting likewise.*

The other seed?

Jesus

It is the seed sown by the evil one, who comes quickly into the field as soon as you go to sleep.

Bartholomew, *sitting beside the others.*

And finally, who are the harvesters, master?

Jesus

The angels, because the barns, my dear ears of corn, are in heaven.

Peter

I will never go to sleep again; I will guard the harvest.

Jesus

You will sleep. — and from this lesson remember above all that you must be patient. So do not angrily snatch out a weed, in case you pull out the wheat at the same time.

Nathaniel, *with wistful longing.*

Wheat! It smells so good when it's freshly ground. I'm hungry.

Jesus

Ask heaven to make this passing cloud drop manna tasting of honey.

Peter

And you believe...?

Jesus

   I do. Peter, you ask.

Peter

       Ask heaven?

Jesus

         Yes.

Peter

And manna will fall?

Jesus

Golden and delicious.

Peter

But ...

Jesus

Ask.

Peter

And yet ...

Jesus

Ask.

Peter

I ...

Jesus

Ask.

Peter, *without conviction.*

Heaven, rain down on us that manna from the sky which once fell on the Hebrews.

A pause.

Nothing is falling.

Jesus

Because you doubted while you prayed. If you truly believed, if you really had faith, you would say to this mountain: "Walk, great boulder!" And Mount Garizim would begin to walk. O men of little faith, go by yourselves to find food. I shall stay here and read — in invisible books. Go on, all of you: Peter, Andrew, James, Nathaniel, Judas.

They leave. Peter, discomfited, trails behind them.

Jesus, *to Peter.*

Yes, Peter, one day my heavenly angels will feed you by fanning you with the wind from their veils; they will satisfy your thirst with the song of their murmuring harps. Your soul will be refreshed with breezes and harmonies. Meanwhile, go and look for food for your body!

The disciples leave, some go towards the town, others to the fields. Jesus is left alone.

I am so tired. But it must be so. I have to go on and on, even though the bushes scratch my hands and the stones are sharp under my feet. But salvation springs from my wounded limbs like wine from crushed grapes, and this satisfying tiredness is the sign that something good will be achieved here. For always, O my God, your wandering son's every fatigue heralds some holy outcome. I sense, because of this suffering — I feel, because I am almost dying of exhaustion, that something great is about to be accomplished here.

The sun is now directly overhead — it is the sixth hour. A flute-like song floats on the gentle breeze towards me. A woman, coming from Sichem. She walks slowly. She is coming to the well. The air is burning.

He has sat down again on the rim of the well.

Now she is close enough for me to see her three-stranded golden necklace, her silken girdle, and her downcast eyes under the long, shading veil ... What beauty my Father has given these Hebrews! I can hear the tinkle of her heavy ankle bracelets. Oh Jacob, how well your daughters know how to balance their water jars gracefully on their heads, as they walk along at an unhurried pace! They walk, smiling silently to themselves, and their shape is one with the shape of the urn, so that their whole body looks like a slender vessel, the upraised arm sketching a handle against the sky ...

At this moment the Samaritan woman appears at the top of the path.

Immortal splendour of this rustic grace! I never tire of watching this gesture, solemn and charming, of our women. I almost fall to my knees when I see it, as I remember that my mother, young, gentle and unknown, unaware of God's love for her, and before she received into her troubled soul the salutation of the angel with golden wings, she too used to carry her pitcher to the well with this very gesture.

This Samaritan woman has erred much, but the vessel, although its divine content has seeped away, still knows itself to be holy by the handle, her bare arm. She is singing of her unworthy profane love.

Scene Five

JESUS, PHOTINE

Photine, *coming down the path singing to herself.*

"Catch these foxes which ruin our vines ...

How strong love is in our hearts!

Give me sweet grapes, for I die.

My beloved is making signs to me ...

Catch these foxes which ruin our vines!

He spoke to me yesterday through the trellis

'Arise, my love; come to me, my beauty!

Winter has fled, the rain is over, flowers are blooming:

The time for singing has come.

They say the turtle dove has already been heard

In our lands:

And already a ripe fig has fallen from the tree.

Arise, my love; come to me, my beauty:

Winter has fled, the rain is over, flowers are blooming'."

Jesus

Her soul is as light as an empty basket.

Photine has arrived at the well, and without looking at Jesus, attaches her pitcher to the rope; she slowly lowers it into the well.

Photine

"I was asleep. Sometimes I sleep,

But even so, my heart keeps watch.

Someone cried to me from outside:

'Open up, heart, flower, star, marvel!'

I replied mischievously

To the dear familiar voice

'I have taken off my linen gown:

How can I open to you, naked as I am?

I have perfumed my feet,

Washed beforehand in the snow:

Should I soil my white feet

On the black tiles, to open to you?'

So I spoke. But I hastened to open:

I have so little strength against him!

But he was gone; I thought I would die,

And when I had rebarred the door

(My fingers left on the bolts

the scent of wild myrrh),

I wept into my auburn hair

And clawed at my face with my nails."

Jesus

Not for an instant has she looked at me.

Photine

"Will he always flee from me, like a shy deer?"

Jesus

Now she is drawing the pitcher back up.

Photine, *turning the wooden wheel which winds up the rope.*

"My beloved — I've sought you — since the dawn,

Without finding you — and now I've found you — it is evening;

But how fortunate! — it's not yet — completely dark:

> *My eyes will still*

> *Be able to see you.*

Your name evokes — all the precious — oils,

Your breath unites — the essence — of all perfumes,

Your slightest words — are composed — of every kind of honey,

> *And your pale eyes,*

> *Of all the skies.*

My heart is melting — like a tender fruit — which has no rind ...

Oh, on this heart — my beloved — this heart which sought you,

Come and rest — gently at first — like a perfume sachet,

> *Then more firmly*

> *Like a seal!"*

Jesus

She is looking at her reflection in the water of her pitcher ...

Photine

"Like a seal of bronze, like a sachet of myrrh!" ...

Jesus

She smiles childishly at herself in this mirror, checks that her makeup is holding well to her eyelashes, and that her hands remain white in spite of the cold water — and the Saviour is here, sitting on the rim of the well!

Photine has put her pitcher back on her shoulder and is leaving the well.

She is going away. This is just like poor Humanity; it brushes against happiness and passes it by!

Photine walks up the path, still murmuring her song.

And suppose I made no sign to this soul! She is going ... And if I let her go? ... Woman!

She turns round and regards him with an insolent air.

I am thirsty, for the sun's rays are very strong. Would you give me a drink?

Photine

I thought that Jews — and this man is evidently a Jew — could have no contact, however slight or distant, with anyone from Sichem. Our bread, to them is pork meat; honey from a bee-hive in Sichem would be bird's blood to them. So, as this pitcher of water is freshly drawn from a Samaritan well, and is carried by a heathen on her impure brow, you should push it away with a gesture of horror, rather than ask ....

Jesus

I am asking you for a drink.

Photine

So your disgust is lessened by your thirst? You know, you would be less polluted by treading on a reptile or touching an insect, than by being helped by someone of my sect.

With spiteful volubility.

No, even if you were to ask me from now until tomorrow, I won't lower my pitcher onto my hand: it is on my shoulder, and there it stays; I'm taking it away.

Farewell, my Eleazar with no gifts, no escort! If you took me for Rebecca, you were mistaken. Yes, you must be very thirsty. But you shall not drink.

Coming back down the path a little way.

Do you see this water, this clear water, this water so clear that even when it is full, the pitcher seems empty, so clear that the drops of freshness which the fine clay of the jar lets seep through like tiny drops of sweat, seem tears or pearls of light! This water, just the clear sound of it makes you thirsty; it's as light as distilled air! But for you, this water is the Law, the harsh Law; for you, this water, so clear and pure, is impure!

Jesus

Woman!

Photine

No, you shan't have any of this water, not even a drop!

Jesus

If you only knew what a sublime present, what a gift of light, God is making to these dark times, or Who it is that asks you for a drink, you would perhaps be well-advised to ask Him for a drink, you, woman, to ask Him.

Photine

You talk in riddles to get me to listen to you.

Jesus

And the water He would have given you, would have been living water.

Photine

I admit, stranger, that your eyes and your voice are pleasing, and that you know, handsome deceitful Jew, how to awaken my interest in talking of this water ... But you have no vessel to draw it up with and the well is deep. What water are you talking about in such a noble, subtle way? Where would you get this water from? Besides, there is no water anywhere better or even as good as this water here. People have been coming here for water for a very long time: this deep well was dug by our ancestor Jacob for his tribe. He and his family drank from it, all of them, as well as their flocks, their camels and their donkeys. It is the most celebrated of all famous wells for its water. You're surely not going to say a word against it? Are you greater than Jacob?

Jesus

I am.

Photine

Oh, if I poured just a little of this water into your cupped hands, you'd soon see!

Jesus

Whoever drinks the water from this well will soon be thirsty again. But those who drink the water which I give them will never be thirsty again, for in them there shall spring a perpetual fount of living water, so that whoever drinks the water I shall give will never need to seek any other water.

Photine

What, never? But now I come to think of it, this must be the water the prophet Elijah knew about, when he stayed so long in the desert without drinking. You are smiling? Oh yes, I know that. You see, I am not entirely ignorant. He stayed there for forty days without drinking – forty! Do you really know his marvellous secret? Sir, please teach it to me. It would save me coming here every day with my pitcher. Water that people could drink without ever becoming thirsty again! Everyone would want some. It could be sold at a very high price.

Jesus

You are only listening to me with ears of flesh. While I want to raise up your soul, it stays below on earth.

Photine

Tell me then about this water which quenches thirst for ever, this spring that never dries up.

Jesus

I will. But first, go and fetch your husband.

Photine

My husband?

Jesus

        Go.

Photine

               But I ...

Jesus

                          This troubles you?

Go and get your husband.

Photine

                          I don't have one.

Jesus

No indeed! You do not have a husband. In saying that, you speak the truth, for the man you are living with is not your husband.

Photine, *recoiling.*

Sir!

Jesus

You're telling the truth. You are no more the wife of the man who shares your bed than you were of the other five.

Photine

Sir!

Jesus

For you have changed your husband five times, shameless woman, but there was no wedding ceremony, no crowd of gently intrusive well-wishers, no torches, ...

Photine

Sir!

Jesus

Not for you the happy hubbub of the banquet, nor the nervousness of the bride carried across the threshold while branches of myrtle are waved above her head.

Photine

Sir, Sir, you must be a prophet!

Jesus

Because I have seen clearly into your disgrace, you now believe that I am a prophet. But truly, woman, I can tell you greater truths than these.

Photine

O Master, please tell me then?

Jesus

What is it you want to know?

Photine

This. You Jews despise us because we pray on this mountain. But I learnt that your ancestors, who are our ancestors too, worshipped there and only there! What should I believe? It's quite clear to the priests and learned men, but for us simple folk, who want to know on which mountain to fall on our knees, it's confusing that there are two. Each priest calls to us praising his own mountain, saying "Pray on ours, it is the oldest!" "No, you can only truly pray on ours!" So as a result we don't pray on either mountain, but stay here below in the valley, where there are flowers which make us forgetful of God.

Jesus

Do not be afraid, innocent soul, for the time is coming — it has come — when people will pray to the Father neither on Garizim nor in Jerusalem. From now on, woman of Sichem, those who truly worship the Father will only worship Him in spirit and in truth. It is not the place where you say your prayers that pleases the Spirit. For the Father is Spirit — God is Spirit and nothing but Spirit. And so it is in the Spirit, always and only in the Spirit, that He is to be worshipped.

Photine

I have lived far from the God whom your voice makes me love. However, I have always held to three beliefs: I believe that one day we will rise from our tombs; I believe we are sometimes visited by angels, and most of all, oh, most of all, I persist in believing that the Promised One will come, and I await with love the Christ, who is called the Messiah!

Jesus, *raising his eyes to heaven.*

Always the lowliest! Oh my Father, I thank you!

To Photine

Tell me, what do you think about this Christ?

Photine

That he will come.

Jesus

Good. And then, once he has come?

Photine

Once he has come ...

Jesus

What do you suppose will happen?

Photine

I suppose he will teach us about everything.

Jesus

Oh my Father, hear these simple words! Woman, you spoke the words I wanted to hear. Raise your head. Look at me. Know that I who speak to you am the one you await: the Messiah!

Photine, *backing away, stammering, she falls to her knees.*

You! ... Christ! ... Emmanuel! ...

Jesus

Jesus.

Photine

My Beloved ...

Jesus

Words fail you now.

Photine

"My beloved — I've sought you — since the dawn,

Without finding you — and now I've found you — it is evening;

But how fortunate! — it's not yet — completely dark:

> *My eyes will still*

> *Be able to see you.*

Your name evokes — all the precious — oils,

Your breath unites — the essence — of all perfumes,

Your slightest words — are composed — of every kind of honey,

And your pale eyes,

Of all the skies.

My heart is melting ..."

Oh dear God! What have I done? What was I saying? For Him, the same song! The same, oh what sacrilege! For Him, the same words I used for ...

Jesus

There is always something of me in words of love. But until they are addressed to me, they are only attempts to express tenderness.

Photine

Master, I worshipped you in the only words I knew.

Jesus

And your homage was sweet to me. I accepted it.

Photine

I'm so ashamed that that song came to my lips in your presence.

Jesus

No, you should not be ashamed. Love of me always comes to live in hearts which have first known earthly love. And so it takes what it finds there, makes use of it, composes other bouquets with the same roses. For all things come back to me. And sooner or later, the perfume, aloe or nard, which the trader thought he had sold for sensual delight, is eventually poured out over my wounded naked feet, and wiped dry with hair once only loosened to seduce.

So do not think that I am shocked by your song. A heart taken by surprise by me cannot recollect itself enough to compose a new song. It is troubled, and in its touching trouble it utters no matter what fragment of a song it knows well, and so the love song becomes a prayer.

Photine

"The one who drinks the water I shall give them will never again be thirsty." Master, it's true — I'm no longer thirsty! For the first time, the very first time, I have drunk your water. Oh, I'd like to weep over your light-bringing hands! How good he is — he holds them out to me ... I have been so, so thirsty, and for so long! This is what I've been seeking, over and over again: living water.

I knew all the false springs. Sometimes I believed I loved, and that, in loving, everything would go better. But I didn't truly love, and I was left with a soul even more thirsty for love. But as soon as I heard of a new spring, the hope of new water and new pathways set me off again, my pitcher in my hands.

Yet it was always the same road, the same cattle grazing in the same place, the same twisted and stunted olive trees, the same blue or grey skies, and it was with the same gesture, but with a wearier soul, that I lowered the pitcher of my desire into the well, always the same well of bitter-tasting sensuality and troubled pleasure ... but no sooner had my lips touched that water, than I would smash my pitcher on the side of the well.

Jesus

Oh Photine, I knew all this!

Photine

And now, I am surrounded by freshness! My soul, startled out of its darkness, has felt rising up within me waves of pure water, the promised spring! Well up, O spring of love, rise up in a jet of faith, and fall again in drops of hope. Sing in me, sing! And instead of shameful dust, envelope my soul with the spray of living water!

Jesus

Now you are finding clever phrases to utter, but they please me less than the tears in your eyes.

Photine

My words have no worth and my eyes are without charm.

Jesus

For me, the loveliest eyes are those full of tears. As for the words, I hear and understand what you say.

Photine

Teach me.

Jesus

Gladly, while I wait. But you will leave when you see my disciples return.

Photine, *gesturing towards her pitcher.*

Before you speak to me, Master, will you not taste the water you asked for?

Jesus

    The only thirst I had was for your salvation.

Photine

It's true! I was naively inviting the River to drink!

Jesus

Each time I drink in a soul, my thirst is quenched.

Photine

I am lying at your feet. I am listening.

Jesus

The air is blue. All is quiet ... I will tell you about the Kingdom of God: how it is lost and how to become worthy of it; I will tell you about the good and bad grain, the vine shoot and the vine ...

Photine

I am listening!

Jesus

I will tell you about the grain of mustard seed, the buried treasure, the diamond that was lost and found again ...

Photine

I am listening!

Jesus

About the dangers of looking back; about the words to choose when forming a prayer, and how the whole flock was left behind in order to look for a lost lamb ...

Photine

I am listening!

Jesus

About the unexpected return of the Master; how the narrow way is better than the broad path, and I will talk to you about my Father.

Photine

I am listening ... !

CURTAIN

TABLEAU TWO

The Gate of Sichem

From behind the curtain comes a hubbub of joyful voices, traders' cries, singing, bursts of laughter. The curtain parts to reveal the market at the town gate of Sichem. We see a large open place onto which converge narrow sloping alleys. Flat-roofed houses with narrow stairs onto the roofs. To the right, Photine's house. At the back, the town gate, a dark, deep archway through which can be glimpsed open country. Above the gate is the house of the gate-keeper, with a little turret from which he can keep a lookout.

Swarming crowds; gaudy costumes; innumerable traders; stalls, shops; piles of sacks, baskets, jars. In the background, a solemn gathering of elders; the town gate is the place for discussions of town business. Children are playing; young men are laughing and amusing themselves by competing to lift heavy stones. Women and girls chatter as they look at the merchandise on offer. The Priest is among the elders near the gate.

Peter and the other disciples are trying to buy provisions, but are being turned away and jeered at by the traders.

Scene One

PETER AND THE DISCIPLES, THE CROWD

Traders' Cries

Grain! Fruit! Milk! Rice! Honey! Salt! Fresh wafers!

Peter

Their shouts are making me even more hungry.

Andrew

Let's go away.

Peter

Over here, madame!

Andrew

It's no good. They're just making fun of us.

Trader

Delicious tartlets!

Andrew, *quickly.*

How much?

A young man running past, *to the traders.*

They're Jews. Charge them extra!

The disciples go away.

Another Trader, *to passing girls.*

Young ladies! Makeup to beautify your eyes!

Another Trader, *to some passing young men.*

Look lads! Reeds from Mérom Marshes, for your arrows!

Peter, *to Nathaniel.*

That old man selling dried figs has a kindly look. Try him ...

Another Trader

Copher, for fingernails!

Andrew, *to Peter.*

I'm dying of hunger.

Peter, *to Nathaniel who has come back.*

Did he accept the price you offered him?

Nathaniel

He told me to get out of his sight.

John

Peter, I'm dying of thirst.

A Trader

Cucumbers from Egypt!

Peter, *resignedly.*

Let's try to buy a fish.

They move backstage.

A young girl in a group, *calling to another as she passes.*

Naomi! What's your boyfriend planning to get you today?

Naomi

Guess!

The Girl

      A cotton bonnet?

Naomi

              No.

Another Young Girl

Some clogs, to clatter merrily as you walk along?

Naomi

            You're joking!

Third Girl

Better than that? A bronze mirror?

Naomi

          Keep guessing!

Fourth Girl

A ring?

Naomi

          An ivory nose-ring!

All, *impressed.*

Ooooh!

Peter, *by the Gate, to a fishmonger.*

This piece of tuna — three shekels?

The Fishmonger

Not to you, it's not! Four!

A Man with birds on his shoulders.

Who wants to see my dear little birds fight?

A crowd gathers around him.

Peter, *to the disciples.*

Let's go!

Andrew

So what have we got, all told?

Nathaniel

A little rice ...

Peter

... dusty.

James

A cheese ...

Peter

... stale.

Andrew

Some fruit ...

Peter

... mouldy.

John, *holding up a small bunch of dried grapes.*

And these grapes!

Peter

By Moses! That's hardly the bunch of grapes from the Promised Land! That won't take two of us to carry it!

To a disciple.

So tell us, keeper of the purse, how much money have we got left?

The Disciple, *showing an empty purse.*

None.

They go towards the gate. They all look at each other.

Peter

Already?

Andrew, *shaking his head.*

> Hmmm.

James, *sotto voce.*

> Judas is stealing from us. We must be careful.

John

When we tell the Master, he just smiles; he looks at him and says "It has to be that he loves money too much".

Peter

Come on!

They make their way towards the gate. As they pass under the arch, there are shouts from the crowd.

The Crowd

The Jews are leaving! Dogs! Pigs! Thieves!

Peter, *quietly to John.*

John, I think there are only ...

The Crowd

> Misers! Skinflints!

Peter

> ... good Samaritans in parables!

Scene Two

THE SAME, WITHOUT THE DISCIPLES. *Azriel is outside Photine's house, on the right.*

Azriel, *to a servant woman who answers the door.*

Is she still at Jacob's Well?

The Servant

> Yes, she's still there.

First Woman, *to another woman.*

Look at Azriel, how anxious he gets when Photine ...

Second Woman

Oh, don't let's talk about Photine!

First Woman

> Life's all honey for that hussy!

Third Woman

Yes, while our days are long and full of honest toil, while we bake bread and spin, her lover compares her to the lilies of the valley, and feeds her salted nuts.

Azriel

> But what could have happened to her?

He calls to the gate-keeper.

Gatekeeper, you can see a long way, perched up there. Can't you see Photine coming along the road?

The Gatekeeper

> No, I can't.

First Woman, *to the second woman.*

Just hark at him, sweetheart. Isn't it irritating?

Second Woman

But you know, my love, they say the scandal is coming to a head. She has lost all shame. They're going to throw her out of town.

Third Woman

Who are?

First Woman

The Elders.

Third Woman

Really?

First Woman

See how quiet they are together, down by the Gate? They are talking about her.

Second Woman

And about time too. She is bad for Sichem and all its inhabitants. Isn't that so, my dear?

First Woman

Yes indeed, my sweet.

Third Woman

If Heaven unleashes its fury on Sichem, it will be because of Photine's alluring eyes.

Fourth Woman

The way she dresses will bring down thunder on our heads!

Fifth Woman

In fact, she's an abominable woman.

Sixth Woman

She certainly is.

First Woman

And God will use her to destroy us.

Second Woman

If she ever looks at us, we'll insult her.

Azriel, *to the servant woman.*

I'm going off to meet her.

The Gatekeeper, *leaning out of his tower.*

Here she is!

Azriel

You can see her?

The Gatekeeper

She's running ... She's waving her arms! ... She's taking a short cut through the vineyards, through the wheatfields ... here she is! ... How fast she's running!

Azriel

Gatekeeper, it can't be Photine!

The Gatekeeper

Yes it is, I can see her clearly... her hair is flying out... she's wild-eyed ... how she's running!

Azriel

It can't be her!

The Gatekeeper

Yes it is! Look!

Photine runs wildly through the archway and comes to a stop, gasping for breath.

Scene Three

Azriel

Ah, it is you! I was trembling ... I was afraid that ... I can't tell you ...
Where have you been? You haven't come from the well? You haven't got a
water jar...

Photine

And yet it's water that I bring.

Azriel

Why were you running?

Photine

People here were thirsty.

Azriel

What? You've come from ..

Photine

The well.

Azriel

Jacob's Well?

Photine

That's what they used to call it.

Azriel

And still call it.

Photine

No.

Azriel

Where's your veil?

Photine

It fell off.

Azriel

Where's your jar?

Photine

My jar?

Azriel

What were you doing? I was looking for you.

Photine

I found myself.

Azriel

Did you have your jar with you when you set off?

Photine

I did.

Azriel

So where have you left it?

Photine

Where I left myself.

Azriel

Why are you tormenting me with this nonsense?

Photine

Poor Azriel!

Azriel

I love you.

Photine

Oh! No, no ... Look, I know all your dreams and thoughts while you're lying in my arms; for in a kiss you lightly touch the whole soul. Nobody knows what is weighing down someone's brow as well as the one whose shoulder is being leant on. Well, please remember, I beg you, everything that I helped you to forget. Those great hopes you threw away? I'm bringing them back to you.

She shouts out.

People!

Azriel

What are you doing?

Photine

Hallo there! You people walking past this Gate, happy and chattering!

Azriel

Photine, it would be better if they did not hear you.

Photine

You women too, who are laughing there in the street!

A Woman

Does she dare to talk to us, that shameless slut?

Azriel

Be quiet! Be careful!

Photine

Elders and Doctors of the Law! Old men! Priests!

An Elder

Silence! We are just discussing you.

Photine

You traders!

A Trader, *scornfully.*

I believe they call you Photine?

Photine

By Jacob's Well there sits a pale young man. He comes from Nazareth, and he spoke to me. He is so gentle, that all at once I began to tremble ... No other man has such eloquence, so powerful yet so natural. He moves his hands like someone opening up a cageful of birds!

The Crowd, *laughing.*

Ha! Ha!

Photine

I believe him to be a prophet. He guessed all my secrets, all my sins! He guessed everything. I'm still overwhelmed by it. Couldn't this man be the Messiah?

A Man

She's mad!

Another man

What's this tale she's telling us?

Another, *laughing.*

Ha! Ha! Ha!

A Trader

Pigeons, who'll buy my pigeons?

Another Trader

Two sparrows going cheap, for a sacrifice!

Photine

I beg you, listen to me!

A Buyer, *to a trader.*

How much is this bag of spices?

The Trader

Twenty shekels.

The Buyer

Do you want to make me as poor as Job?

Photine

A young man is sitting by Jacob's Well. He is called Jesus. He is returning from Judea. At first I refused to give him the water he asked me for. But then, standing there in his cloak, he spoke to me words from heaven about this water ... !

A Woman, *to a trader.*

What lovely necklaces!

Another Woman

Where do they come from?

The Trader

Phoenicia.

Photine

Why won't you believe that this is the Messiah?

A Young Man

The Messiah? He'll come when our bones are rotting.

Photine

Wretched people, listen to me! I'm bringing tremendous news!

A Trader

She's so tiresome.

Another Trader

Keep quiet!

Photine

I can't keep quiet any longer!

The First Trader

No! Enough of your shouting!

Photine

I can't keep quiet any longer ... I know that I must keep shouting, even though you reject me and trample on me. It is my duty to come and cry out to the crowd.

Beside Jacob's Well there sits a young man! His hair is the colour of ripe corn; each of his lovely eyebrows reminds you of the rainbow with God's promise to the world.

He stands serenely under an invisible canopy, holding an invisible palm. His calmness would mark him out among thousands, and he is the One I have been waiting for!

His gracious bearing makes one think of a summer breeze carrying a distant melody, wafting through perfumed bushes, with the sound of the flute blending with the scent of flowers in the warm air.

His gentleness is godlike, it's ... it's like a dove's white feather falling into milk!

A Trader

She's stirring up the crowd ...

Another Trader

           ... And distracting the customers.

A Man, *bitterly, addressing the traders.*

Oh yes, what do the greatest hopes and the deepest longings matter, as long as people can carry on buying and selling!

Another Man, *to the Priest who is approaching, drawn by the noise.*

Someone is talking to us about the Christ!

The Priest

           Who is?

Photine

           I am!

The Priest

You've got a nerve! Speaking about the Christ? Do you even know who that is? The only person who can speak about these matters is the devout man who knows all the ancient oracles, the sayings of the holy prophets, the written promises ... things that women know absolutely nothing about.

Photine

You would do well, priest, to support what I say. For it is written: "When God arrives on the mountain, the blind shall see the lame dance, and the deaf will hear the dumb rejoicing".

The Priest

This is actually a text she is rephrasing for us!

An Old Man

What? This ignorant woman?

A Young Man

She seems to be in ecstasy!

Another Young Man

Her lips have been touched with coals of fire.

Photine

"In place of their hearts of stone, I am sending my people true hearts of flesh, so that henceforth they will walk in my ways, and will be my people, and I will be their God."

The Priest

These were the words of Ezekiel in his ecstasy. She must have read them somewhere.

Azriel

She can't read.

The Priest

Then how does she know the sacred texts?

Photine

"How beautiful upon the mountain are the feet of those who bring good news ..."

The Priest

Isiah's prophecy!

Photine

"And you, little town of Bethlehem, what other city ever saw your splendours?"

The Priest

Ah! Be quiet!

Photine

"Nazareth! Your name is wreathed in flowers!"

The Priest

Only the books of Moses enlighten souls.

Photine

Well then, know that it says in the Book of Numbers: "The oracle of Bâlaam of Peor: 'Israel, from your soil comes a sceptre and in your sky is a star!'"

The Priest

This woman knows the Five Books better than a man!

Photine

And know that it says in Deuteronomy ...

Different Voices

It's a miracle! It's false ! It's the Christ! Do you think so? No!

Photine

And if it is him! Come and see him!

A Voice from the crowd

Remember all the false prophecies.

Another Voice

So many Messiahs have been found before.

Photine

But if it is him!

A Trader

No, no!

Photine

But if it is him!

A Young Man

Oh well, in that case ...

The Priest

But just supposing he were the Christ, how could his great pure soul talk to your soul?

Photine

His soul stoops down to mine.

The Priest

Go off and sprinkle your doorstep with perfume, and sit there preparing the snares of your eyes for this evening.

Photine

Don't think you'll upset me with that kind of talk. I deserve all that you're saying.

Azriel

How humble this proud beauty has become! There's certainly something divine at work here.

Photine, *kneeling in the centre of the square.*

I confess my sins, beating my breast, and beg you all to forgive me.

A Woman, *raising her up.*

Photine!

Photine

Yes indeed, I am a prophetess very unworthy of him! But the gentle saviour who has come to us today loves precisely those whom no one loves. He loves those you hold in scorn, those whose sufferings are ignored because of their lowly position: impoverished people, wretched animals, beaten dogs, sad donkeys, publicans, tax collectors, prostitutes!

Various people, *shouting.*

Make her shut up! She's a sinner! Stop her talking!

Photine

Jesus has forgiven me my sins.

A Woman, *running to her from out of the crowd.*

Would he forgive all my sins too?

Photine

You can be sure of it. If a reed is bent, he won't cut it down; if a lamp splutters and blackens its wick, he won't blow hard on it. But, so that the reed can sway again and offer a safe perch to the birds, he will gently set it straight. So that the lamp's flame may rise brightly again, he will gently raise its wick with a needle.

The Priest

Oh, these appeals to the heart are more damaging than vinegar to the teeth or smoke to the eyes!

A Young Man

How lovely she is at this moment!

A Second Young Man

It's because the Spirit has breathed on her.

A Third Young Man

No, it's because she is beautiful.

A Fourth Young Man, *trying to draw Photine away towards a small group of convinced people.*

Come! Some of us already ...

Photine

No! I'll only leave if half the town comes with me.

A Child

I'll come!

Photine, *moving through the crowd.*

You whose homes people cannot visit without spending hours purifying themselves afterwards, I'm talking to you. You who are treated with more disdain than showmen and strolling minstrels; you who are excluded from every privilege, vile pagans, heretics, drunkards, unholy people — Samaritans, in a word, for this word says it all and has become a name of scorn.

Follow me towards this Christ, you who are the poor of this world and shut out from the next, for this Christ is your Christ! Those who have never known shame or pain, the strong and joyful, do not own this Christ — he is yours!

The Priest

The Christ is a conqueror who will come in glory.

Photine

He is a poor man who asks for something to drink.

The Priest

Crowned with stars, he will arrive out of the sky, his path marked by lightning flashes, and riding on the wings of the wind!

Photine

He has come along the valley path. His brow is not star-crowned but his soul is full of stars.

The Priest

He will come to cry: "There is only the law"!

Photine

He comes to sigh: "There is only faith".

The Priest

He will be the warrior who reclaims the earth!

Photine

He is the peaceful enemy of war, the destroyer of destruction and the death of death.

The Priest

Do we even know where this prophet has come from? The true Christ will be a descendant of David — and of the priesthood.

Photine

His ancestry will be traced back to David. Until it is, he is known to have come from a lowly background. His hands have held tools. Angels have kissed the wood shavings caught in his hair as he worked in an obscure workshop. God though he is, he has obediently fashioned yokes and scales, and as he worked, he has thought of your burdens as he planed the yokes, and dreamed of justice as he levelled the scales.

A Man

Let's go to him!

The Priest

It is a false Christ.

The Man

Maybe. But I will follow all the false Christs, for fear of missing the true one.

A Woman

Yes, lead us to him! Leave behind these hearts of stone.

Photine

No! I will not leave unless the whole town comes with me.

A Man, *mockingly.*

A Christ who comes to forgive sinners!

Photine

His words make silences in people's hearts ...

Another Man, *also mockingly.*

... and who gossips with women beside wells.

Photine

His gestures bring holy peace to souls.

A Trader

So, he is handsome when he speaks?

Photine

He is resplendent! No one has ever spoken like this man. He says: " The first shall be last ... Those who suffer will smile ... Those who rise high are on the edge of a precipice ... Blessed are the sorrowful, for they will be joyful ... Blessed are the weary, for they will find rest".

A Trader

Look, a crowd is growing around her.

Photine

I am going to shout out all he said in the streets.

She leaves, followed by the crowd.

First Old Man

And she is!

A Trader, *looking after her.*

Soon there will be thousands!

Another Trader, *shouting despairingly after the crowd.*

Why have you left your workshops?

A Third Trader

What can we do? We can't let her go on like this.

The Voice of Photine, *off-stage.*

He says, "You who are weak will be strong".

First Trader

Don't let her say such things!

The Voice of Photine, *further away.*

He says, "You will judge those who judge you".

An Old Man, *furiously.*

That's it!

Another Old Man

What's to be done?

The Priest

We must get the Romans.

To a trader.

You, go quickly.

He explains in a whisper what to say. Just audible are the phrases:

... danger to public order ... the populace getting overexcited ...

The Voice of Photine, *outside.*

He also says: "I tell you in truth, my Inheritance is for the disinherited".

A Trader, *terrified.*

Do you hear these words raining down on the town?

The Priest, *to the man he is sending.*

Tell them to bring soldiers. Say it's civil war if it isn't stopped.

The Voice of Photine, *getting closer.*

He says, "Of two paths, choose the narrower".

Priest, *to the trader.*

Go and get the Romans.

The trader runs out.

Photine, *coming back on stage with a much larger crowd.*

He also says: "All knowledge is a delusion. My Kingdom belongs to the poor in spirit". He says ...

A Man who is following her, *overcome, staggering, intoxicated.*

Listen everyone! Keep close to her. These are words no one could make up. Only a God could inspire these golden words. What else does he say, Photine?

Photine

He says: "Be gentle. Be understanding. Be accepting. Smile. Look kindly on others. Behave towards others as you would like others to behave towards you. This is all the law and all the prophets. Share the sufferings of others" ... what else? New words, especially one which keeps coming back: "love ... love ...loving... When we love, we know heaven. To be loved by the Father, love your neighbour.

Give everything for love's sake. Share your bread with the friend who comes at night and asks for it. If while you are bringing your offering to God, you remember that your brother has a complaint to make against you, go and make peace with him and embrace him before you return to your prayers. But such love is not enough. Even pagans can love their brothers. It's not asking much to love those who love you: love those who oppress and insult you. Forgive seventy times seven.

To worship me, love those who don't want you to love them. If such a person beats you, don't cry out against them but pray for them. If someone takes your coat, give them two shirts. Love ungrateful people as if they were your only son. If you love your enemies, you will be my friends. Love greatly, so that much may be forgiven you. Keep on loving. Love always. Love in spite of everything. Love each other dearly. Give up your lives for love. I myself will show you how to love, one day ... Love! Have only love in your heart. Love each other."

All, *falling to their knees.*

What is this? What teaching is this?

Cries, excitement.

The King, the Son of David! The Christ! The King of Heaven! Let's follow her.

They get up, full of enthusiasm, and rush after Photine to leave the town, but they are brutally pushed back by soldiers who are entering it. A centurion appears.

Scene Four

THE SAME, THE CENTURION, SOLDIERS

The Centurion

What's this? Seditious shouts? Away with you all! ... Who is this you are acclaiming as king? What are you all doing gathered round this woman? ... Seize her!

Photine, *as they bind her hands.*

All is lost! And just when I was leading them away!

The Centurion, *to the grumbling crowd.*

Didn't you hear me? No groups! No mutterings! All of you, get moving!

To the traders.

As for you, go back to your counters.

To Photine.

You agitator, you were inciting them against Caesar, no doubt, and against taxes. What were you saying to them?

Photine

I was talking about ...

The Centurion, *to the soldiers.*

Tighten those cords.

Photine

About forgiveness and pity, about charity and love ...

The Centurion

And after that ...

A Man, *swiftly.*

That's all!

Another Man, *also swiftly.*

Nothing else.

The Priest

She was also speaking about the Messiah.

The Crowd, *indignantly.*

Oh!

The Centurion

So, you have come to denounce her, have you? Rome thanks you ...

Laughing, to the soldiers.

It seems she was announcing the Avenger, the Messiah, the one who will be Emperor of the Jews, who will fight the Romans? Well, she's wrong to do so, for this will probably not please Pilate. Let's go.

Photine, *aside.*

All is lost.

The Priest

To encourage them to riot, she said she had seen the Christ very near here. And do you know who this crazy woman has the nerve to call the Christ? An obscure fanatic, no doubt plotting trouble, a beggar from Nazareth.

The Centurion

Ah! I'm glad you said that. A beggar from Nazareth? ... I know what this is all about.

To his soldiers

It's that man, you know, the simpleton who is supposed to have cured lepers, the Galilean. We had been told he was in this area.

The Priest

You must have received orders about him.

The Centurion

He's called Joshua, isn't he, or Jesus?

The Priest

That's him.

The Centurion

So, it's Jesus! When I think I was about to ... But that doesn't matter now. He's no threat, that one.

To the soldiers

It's nothing. It's only Jesus. Untie her!

Photine, *released at once.*

Gracious Heavens!

The Centurion

He's a poor Jew prone to melancholy. I myself saw him do a crazy thing in Jerusalem, about a month ago. I was on guard at Fort Antonia, from where we can watch everything that goes on in the temple. From my post I saw someone wearing a flowing white robe, and said to myself: "It's some Essene come from En-Gadi. He's preaching, I can see that from the movements of his sleeve". Twelve dark robes were following the white robe.

The little group, talking together, came to the place where pious Jews, to honour their God, sit at little tables changing money, usually using false weights. They sell everything at this extraordinary temple: salt, oil, live animals. Old bits of strap and cord lie around on the ground. Suddenly I saw the man in white garments pick up one of these cords and twist it round; I saw him whipping all the traders thronging the place. And all these fat traders, even those suffering from gout, were fleeing, whipped by him, like a herd of donkeys. He kept on whipping them furiously. And the people cheered.

This man is no threat to the Empire. He doesn't allow the temple to be made into a vile bazaar, but he says "Render unto Caesar that which is Caesar's".

The Priest

Didn't you hear what the woman was saying?

The Centurion, *laughing and getting back on his horse.*

I'd rather not hear her!

The Priest, *trying to hold him back.*

Listen to her!

The Centurion

I've got better things to do.

The Priest

What kind of things?

The Centurion, *mockingly.*

Reading my favourite author in a shady spot. As I read, the shadow of a fig leaf, like a large trembling hand moving across the page, underlines with its blue finger some lovely line of Horace.

The Priest

But ...

The Centurion, *coldly.*

Above all, see to it that no one comes to disturb me.

To the people.

You are allowed this Christ. He's no danger to us.

Going out, to a soldier.

You know, the handsome carpenter with blond hair? That one will never upset the world! Let's go!

Scene Five

THE SAME, WITHOUT THE CENTURION AND HIS SOLDIERS

Photine

And now, let's run!

Murmurs in the crowd

A Man

Oh no!

Photine

What's wrong?

Second Man

A king who flatters Caesar won't be my king.

Third Man

Is this how the Son of David sets us free?

Fourth Man

He advises us to pay taxes?

Fifth Man

He accepts Tiberius?

Photine

Lord, Lord, just listen to these sad souls! What kingdom did you think I was talking to you about? You're concerned about Caesar, about the Empire? Try to understand what is being said to you. You, who will always be Samaritans, just think about the only true kingdom, the secret kingdom, none of whose provinces will ever be seized by any prince.

Sooner or later you are bound to be eaten up, so what does it matter which wild beast comes creeping up on you in the dark, whether it's the Jewish fox or the Roman she-wolf? Without knowing the name of the master that chance will impose, disdainfully give Caesar his due.

All

Yes, but ...

A Man

But the kingdom?

Photine

It is not of this world, for it was founded by a God, not a king.

A Second Man

Where shall we find it, this kingdom that is not real?

Photine

A little in yourselves, at first. Then completely in heaven.

Several Voices

In ourselves?

Photine, *going from one to the other.*

That is where the seed is, and from it will grow the immense tree.You only have to want it and the kingdom's reign begins — for everyone! For everyone! A little love, a little faith, and you will see what a beautiful kingdom it is! For you — and you — and you!

You, stone-cutter, you will suffer less, for in the dark of the mask which protects your eyes, you will glimpse some tiny gleams from the future beams of light ... Engraver, your fingers will be refreshed by the wingbeats of the tiny silver cherubim you are engraving ... Carpenter, as you saw up cedarwood, cypresses and acacia for panelling alcoves, you will bless the cracks in the wall of your shed because a tuft of hyssop is growing there ... Weavers, you will pity those you weave for ... Stitchers, the more you sew useless braid onto frivolous clothes, the more you will smile, like philosophers.

Each one will find joy in their humble calling. Potter, you will glaze your clay with love. Shepherds, you will tend your bees more gaily. Basketmakers, you will whistle as you weave your baskets.

The Priest

But the kingdom of heaven is only a hope.

Photine

Have you anything better to suggest?

Cries from everyone

Yes! Let's follow her! The Christ! Perhaps! The Kingdom! Let's take our instruments! Let's sing! All of us! A psalm!

A Trader, *to Photine.*

I'm just going because I'm curious. I don't believe in it.

Photine

Come anyway.

Azriel

I'm going out of boredom, without any hope, just to be doing something!

Photine

Come anyway.

A Young Man

For me, it's you I love. If I follow you, it's because you're beautiful.

Photine

Come anyway. Follow, all of you, plucking olive branches on the way. I don't mind why you come, as long as you come.

The Priest

Oh well! I'll go along as well. Perhaps this man will found a new religion and name me high priest!

Photine

As we go, let's sing the psalm to the Eternel One. Let's start from *"Let us sing to the psaltery ..."*

The Whole Crowd, *singing loudly and enthusiastically.*

"Let us sing to the psaltery, emblazoned with gold, coral and mother of pearl; let us sing to the harp and the flute, and to the ram's-horn trumpet!"

The crowd surges behind Photine into the archway of the town gate and the psalm they sing resounds far into the countryside.

The Crowd

"Let the earth and all its people dance in honour of Him who comes to judge the world ... All the sea ... and all ..."

CURTAIN

TABLEAU THREE

The Saviour of the World

We are back at Jacob's Well. Jesus is sitting on the well's rim. The sun is about to set; the golden sky is infused with rose.

The disciples are in a group a little way away from the Master. They are finishing the frugal meal that they managed to acquire with their somewhat random purchases. Sitting or lying on the ground, they form a circle round a small dying fire from which rises, straight up into the calm air, a thin blue thread. They are whispering together, occasionally shooting a surreptitious glance at Jesus. They are not happy. Jesus is lost in thought.

Scene One

JESUS, THE DISCIPLES

Peter, *in a low voice, indignantly.*

To this woman!

Andrew, *likewise.*

He was speaking to her!

Peter

I would never dare to criticize him ... But let's admit it: he is sometimes strangely imprudent.

Andrew

And why is he fasting, when everyone else is eating?

Peter

It's to amaze us that he hasn't eaten.

Jesus

That is not the reason, Peter.

John

He can hear us.

Peter

I spoke too loudly.

Nathaniel, *more quietly.*

But why fast?

Peter

I imagine it's to prove to us that he can live without nourishment.

Jesus

I am nourished by food that you know nothing of.

Peter, *lowering his voice.*

Someone must have brought him a meal.

John

Angels may care for him without being seen.

Jesus

Doing the will of the One who sent me, that is the secret food which nourishes me.

Peter, *even more quietly, in an exasperated voice.*

That was why we came this way ...

John

... even though to reach Galilee ...

Peter

It would have been better to go via the valley of Sharon ...

Nathaniel

Yes, or across the plain of Jordan!

Andrew

But to come through Samaria! Horrors! Just taste this bread! It's like granite!

He throws it a long way away.

Cursed town!

Peter

Is it worth this trouble to go among these ignorant people, who are full of hatred, hardened and made spiteful by their sufferings?

Jesus

It is among these people that it is necessary for me to go, so that is where I am going.

John

Let's speak more quietly.

James

It's his idea. He will get us massacred.

John

But he is putting himself at risk too.

Peter

What good will it do? What has he come to look for? What's he doing at this well? Who is he hoping to preach to? He's only found this woman to listen to him. As you know, I never criticize him, but if he wanted to win over these people, he should have found an advocate worthy of being listened to!

John

Pure hands alone can sow the seed of the Idea.

Peter

But a courtesan!

James

They will have stoned her as soon as she stood up to preach!

Peter

Well, if I ever wanted to win over a town ...

James

You?

Peter

I would make enquiries first. I would go and see the important people, the priest at the altar, the money-changers at their tables. Everyone is useful according to their importance. I would convince someone important. There! That's how I would win over a town.

Andrew, *shaking his head,*

Talking to that woman was no use at all.

Peter

Sometimes he really seems to be almost ridiculously unreasonable. Just think, he's chosen the least important city of the least important people, and in the whole city, a woman, and of those, the least important.

Jesus

You must get used to the fact that, with me, the last come first, and the lowest come the highest.

Peter

He hears everything. All right, I'll keep quiet then.

He gets up and goes off to look at a field of wheat.

Jesus

No!

James

What are you saying "No!" to?

Jesus

To what Peter is thinking.

Peter, *turning round, astonished.*

Lord! ...

John, *crying our suddenly.*

> I'm dying of thirst!

Andrew

Yes, those heathens have played a cruel trick on us. They've put too much salt in the rice.

Nathaniel

But how can we drink?

Andrew

> We've got nothing to draw up water with.

John

Well, that woman left behind ...

James

> What?

John

> Her water jar!

Peter

Her disgusting water jar? It's an object of scandal and dread! Don't even touch it!

John, *both hands round the jar.*

> It feels cool. And I'm very thirsty.

Peter

I wouldn't drink that foul water for anything in the world.

John

> Is it foul?

Peter

Doubly! For that water will taste of vice and impiety too.

John

That's too bad! I'm too thirsty to care!

He drinks from the jar.   Oh!

Nathaniel

Well?

John,

      Taste it!

Nathaniel, *after tasting it.*

            Oh!

Andrew

              What?

Nathaniel, *passing him the jar.*

                Taste it!

Andrew

                    Oh!

James

                       What is it?

Andrew

Taste it!

James

        Has a heavenly pearl dissolved in this water?

Nathaniel

It's like honey.

Andrew

      No, like flowers.

John

            Just tasting it makes me weep.

Peter

What can she have left in her jar when she left?

Jesus

> She left in this jar the cares of a foolish heart,
>
> The cruel pride of being a living, lovely snare,
>
> Her heavy burden of sin, her worst nightmares,
>
> Her idle and wicked pleasures, her frivolous laughter,
>
> Her thoughtless singing, her sighs for unworthy reasons,
>
> All her soul's ills, all of them!

Peter

And it is these bad things that make the water taste so good?

Jesus

> The water from this jar, that you find so delicious,
>
> Is not flavoured with golden honey drops
>
> > And white essence of lilies.
>
> Its taste, which savours of infinity,
>
> Is what comes to me when all the faults of a life
>
> > Lie forgotten at my feet!

Peter, *drinking in his turn from the jar.*

Where can I find words for such freshness? My lips hear your voice which my ears were drinking!

He sets down the jar.

But just now, when I was looking at the field over there, when you said "No!", what was I thinking of?

Jesus

The harvest. You were comparing this field to my thought, and thinking of the long, sad sleep of the sown seed.

Peter

Yes. It's still four months to the harvest.

Jesus

And I said, "No!"

Peter

     Why?

Jesus

       Look up.

Peter

         Why, Lord?

Jesus

Look up. The harvest is glowing bright. Someone has sown it for you, now take up your sickle. One person sows, another reaps, yet the joy — yes, this is a good injustice — must always be the same for both the reaper and the sower. You have been called to reap, but others have sown the seed. Their ears of corn are now ripe. Look!

Peter

It's true that over there, beneath the red evening sky, the fields seem to be whitening for the harvest.

John

       The whiteness is moving!

The Crowd, *in the distance*

... on the harp ... on the psaltery ...

Nathaniel

       And you can hear ...

Peter

What sort of harvest is this which moves along singing?

They have all climbed up onto the bank and are staring into the distance.

Andrew

It's the town which is coming!

John

A white stream of townspeople is flowing through the dark archway of the town gate.

Peter

It's as if a powerful hand was squeezing the walls, making the people burst through onto the road.

The Crowd

... let us sing also to the flute ...

Peter

And who can that woman be who proudly walks in front?

Jesus, *sitting without moving on the rim of the well.*

You must get used to the fact that with me, the last shall be first.

The Crowd, *coming closer.*

And in honour of he who comes ...

John

                                        Listen, listen!

Peter

Master, I humbly beg your forgiveness for my doubts.

The Crowd, *coming closer.*

                    Let the Earth and all its people dance!

John

Oh, do get up! Come and see!

Nathaniel

                            The fields are dazzling!

Peter

Where on earth did they get all those roses?

James

      Come and see!

Jesus

          I do see them.

Peter

               But your eyes are shut.

Jesus

In my heart I saw them coming a long time ago.

The Crowd, *getting closer still.*

          The sea and all that therein is ...

Andrew

They're getting closer!

Voice of Photine, *singing very close to them now.*

May the mountains move, and the rivers stretch their arms far from their their broad beds, to clap their green hands in joy!

Peter

That soaring voice!

Jesus

        Ah! Photine, is that you?

Photine, *appearing on top of the bank, breathless, dishevelled, covered in flowers gathered as she ran along, her eyes blazing.*

Yes, Lord, and the whole town is with me!

She has been preceded by an excited crowd of children who race down the paths from every direction, waving olive branches as they slide down the bank. She is followed by the crowd which swarms on to the stage and rushes shouting towards Jesus. Jesus stands up. The crowd comes to an abrupt halt and is silent.

Scene Two

Jesus

Photine!

Photine, *beside herself.*

They've all come! A rapturous crowd. I don't remember any more what I said; they've followed me! I ran. I've lost my bracelets. I'm laughing. Isn't it true that all the lepers will be cured? If you had seen us! Here are the young girls ... here are the beggars with flowers in their crutches. The whole way we were singing and running; no centurion could have stopped us!

Here, I've picked this wild rose for you ... Come nearer, old man, he'll touch and heal your wound ... The children danced ahead of the procession. And here, look, my hands are bleeding from breaking off so many green branches for them! ... All Sichem's houses are deserted! The first to want to come was this little one here ... This young man was not a believer when he set off, but just by following us he's lost his doubts, yes, just by making the effort to come! ... The traders thought only of their lost trade, and the priest argued with me. But I, I answered him, and I felt it was your Spirit speaking through me.

Ah! How happy I am to breathe in the scent of the grass! I don't recognise my voice any more in the evening air. As for the traders, we shouldn't blame them. The women were very good right from the start. I am laughing! I'm so happy! You will have to permit us to kiss your long woollen cloak, as we have come to worship you.

(To the women.) Come here!

I'll tell you their names. You who see everything, you can see that they've all come, and you will recognise them without having known them. This is Thamar, this is Penninah. People are still arriving; they're in all the fields nearby. It's a huge crowd. I'm rather out of breath. I'm going to cry. I am so happy.

Jesus

You have won over the town for me.

Photine

Oh no! You alone struck the blows! If the victory is great, it's not because I, a prophetess chosen from among fallen women, took it on myself to convey your message there. It happened because you, O Holy Silent One, were watching the town from here; your eyes laid invisible siege to its walls.

I didn't conquer the town for you, you the only conqueror whose robe remains white as snow, you the tender enemy, the noble warrior, the pure-hearted victor. The town surrendered to you. Your humble servant could not have been any help. I am nothing in all this: I bring you the keys of the town, that's all. I, who am nothing, bring you the keys to all these hearts on the cushion of my own heart.

A Man

Like the huge red muzzle of a lioness poised over a lamb, startled by its whiteness, the monstrous town is silent around you.

Another

The crowd which used to shout and rebel now holds its breath.

A Woman

And open-mouthed, listens to you.

Photine

                                                    You could hear a beetle fly.

A Woman

Speak to us, give us water to drink from holy springs!

Photine

See how all these olive branches tremble in every hand, even though there is no breeze.

Azrael

Who is this man whose very silence makes me tremble and quiver like a wing? Was my soul only pretending to be asleep?

A Man

We are that despised ignorant people, idolaters, that the Jews have told you about ...

Jesus

I am your good shepherd.

Another Man

We are the black sheep, mangy and mean, from the cursed sad flock.

Jesus

You are my sheep. No flock can be less dear to me because it comes from this or that sheepfold. I shall make my voice heard in every meadow; I shall gently take down the wooden fences that separate you; the posts and planks will collapse on the grass, until all the black and white sheep are gathered under my light shepherd's crook, and there is only one sheepfold in the world, and one shepherd.

A Young Man

I feel as if his words are baptising me!

A Woman

Please touch my tears.

Another Woman

Please bless my little boy.

An Old Man

Even if they tell me my last hour has come, I am ready now!

A Young Girl

Oh! I didn't dare to hope he would look at me!

A Man

How his head is bent in sympathy!

A Woman, *coming forward and prostrating herself.*

Until now I was hiding in the crowd, afraid of a severe look from your eye.

Jesus

I have already raised up the woman taken in adultery.

A Trader

You whipped my colleagues from the temple. Will you forgive me for having neglected true riches in my desire to obtain the treasures of this world?

Jesus

It was only from the temple that I chased away the traders.

The Drunkard

Will you forgive me, O prophet of the living water, for not having been content to drink only the pure water which your Father gave us to drink?

Jesus

I changed water into wine at the wedding in Cana.

The Priest

Can this be the Christ, someone who allows prostitutes and drunkards to follow him?

Jesus, *angrily.*

I will answer you, wretched man.

At this moment the children begin to sing and dance.

Peter, *speaking severely to a woman.*

Take these children away!

Jesus, *suddenly calm again.*

Why take them away? I forbid you to. What! Just for singing a childish round? Let the little ones come to me ... Photine, bring me the two that are hiding in the folds of your dress.

Photine, *to the children.*

Come here!

Priest

So, you are not answering me?

Jesus

I am preparing my reply.

Photine, *to the children.*

Do you see this gentleman?He's a very great prophet, the one we've been waiting for, the one we were always talking about. He doesn't make bears eat up little children, like the prophet Elijah in the story. He just places his hands on their curly heads in blessing.

Jesus

Oh, what bright, fresh eyes they have! Have eyes like this and you will be sure of entering the kingdom of heaven.

To the children.

Will you sing again the round you were singing while you danced?

To the disciples.

No one is to scold them!

A Child

When we played for you

Joyful dancing tunes,

You did not dance.

Another Child

When we played for you

Sad weeping tunes,

You did not weep.

Jesus

Peter, you are quite wrong to frown like that; their little song has given me my answer to the priest. For it surely mocks the men of today, who, alas, no matter what one does, are never satisfied? John the Baptist arrived, rough, aggressive and alone; weather-beaten, clad in skins and eating locusts for his food; his eyes blazing at sinners. You said: "He's a furious madman!"

Jesus comes along, eating, drinking, smiling, quick to forgive, and you say of him: "He's just a pleasure-seeker!" Ungrateful, unbelieving race! I was almost going to ... But now these children have sung, and their song was the best reply. Wisdom has come through the mouths of the children.

A Trader

This man, who loves us and speaks to us like this, is truly the Saviour of the world!

A Man, *crying out.*

Yes, this man is truly the Saviour of the world!

Photine

He makes you feel like dying!

Azriel

        Now I know what to do with my life!

A Young Man

His finger writes on my soul in letters of light!

Another

A wonderful bridge now arches from his heart to mine; I feel it trembling.

A Man, *guided by Photine up to Jesus.*

I am blind.

Jesus

   See!

Another Man, *carried by servants.*

       I am crippled.

Jesus

          Walk!

The Crowd

A miracle!

Jesus, *to another.*

     And you, old man, speak!

The Old Man

I was dumb!

A Man, *coming forward.*

My heart had ceased to feel anything. But already, just now, I almost wept ... but then, I couldn't. It's hard to weep.

Jesus

Weep!

Peter

How glad we are to see you performing miracles like this, Lord!

Jesus

You will perform them too.

Andrew

Who will? We will?

Jesus

One day I shall have to send you out ... and then you too will perform miracles.

Peter

We will? What joy!

Jesus

It is not for this that you ought to rejoice, but because your names are written in heaven.

Photine

Night will fall here when your shining presence has gone. Please don't leave us too soon to our sad darkness. Stay!

Stay with us, Lord! We need to hear

More of your good news.

Our guest is the son of God!

Must he leave us in tomorrow's dawn?

An Old Woman

> You must come to my house
>
> To rest after your labours.
>
> You really cannot leave
>
> Before you have tasted our figs!

A Courtisan

> Stay and speak to us! Your words fall
>
> Like flowers sprinkled over our heads.
>
> Tears will replace the golden chains
>
> That decorate my cheeks!

A Woman

> And when you return, exhausted
>
> From visiting the sick,
>
> I will have wine ready to revive you,
>
> Flavoured by my pomegranates.

Photine

> We will tenderly respect
>
> Your daily routine.
>
> The town will fall silent
>
> During your hours of prayer.

A Woman

> At twilight, when voices sound
>
> Loud and strange,
>
> You will come to sit for a moment
>
> On all the doorsteps!

A Young Woman

> The breezes here are cool, so if
>
> Your white cloak slips from your shoulders,
>
> One of us will put it on again, without disturbing
>
> You while you preach.

Photine

> And you will feel the whole time
>
> That you are speaking to our souls;
>
> The children's hair beneath your hands
>
> The women's hair beneath your feet.

As each woman speaks, she comes to kneel in front of Jesus and lays down her olive branch or her wreathed staff. As Photine finishes speaking they all lean forward and unloose their hair at his feet.

Jesus

I will stay with you for two days; I cannot stay longer. For two days I wish to rest with you.

A Woman

And then you will set off again on your journey, with its sublime fatigues.

Photine

And when you leave us, and climb the heights of the Mountains of Ephraim which rise into our skies, from time to time you will just be able to see, at the far edge of Jezreel's flowery meadows, what looks like a little flock of sheep with what might be its shepherd on the hillside opposite. The bright cluster of houses is Nazareth, and the shepherd is its synagogue.

Jesus

Nazareth! I used to run about your alleys as a child! But of all cruel towns, you will be the cruellest to me. You will not listen to the whole of my preaching; you'll say: "Oh, it's the carpenter's son!" And so it will be my own people who are most opposed to me, and when I seek for brothers, I shall discover, weeping — a moving symbol of my destiny —

that my kindest brothers are here among the people of Samaria! But it is said that no one is a prophet in his own country! May the will of my Father be done!

Cries from Everyone

Hosannah! Glory to the Christ! Come to our town, come!

Jesus

Was I wrong to come amongst these pagans, Peter?

Photine, *indicating the darkening sky.*

Night is falling. This day is ready to die. But it will never die. It will live for ever. When the olive trees and the fig trees are dust, when the well of Jacob runs dry, even then, always flowing from the valley, past mountain and hillside, the Living Water will flood the world.

Jesus

And you, Photine, you will be seen through the centuries coming slowly down the path, your water jar poised on your head. And when in the distant future people try to picture me, either Mary of Magdala or the woman of Samaria will always be beside me. And you may be proud that sometimes your auburn hair may be confused with her blonde tresses.

The Priest

So be it! He is the Son of God! I'm willing to believe it. So will he rebuild our temple?

Jesus

      No!

The Priest

      But you will appoint priests.

Jesus

      Not yet.

The Priest

Well, a High Priest, at least.

Jesus

No.

The Priest

Do you wish us to honour you yourself with this title?

Jesus

Oh no! no!

The Priest

But we could embellish your robe with embroidery.

Jesus

No.

The Priest, *pointing to his chest.*

And you won't wear the glittering insignia with its twelve gems, here?

Jesus

I have my twelve disciples.

A Young Man

But which temple shall we choose for you, we who love you?

Photine

Lakeside meadows in flower, blue hillsides!

Another Young Man

What throne will he ascend to preach from?

Photine

The rim of a well, the wooden seat of a boat.

The Priest

But how can we please the Lord, then?

Jesus

Only actions please God.

The Priest

But surely we will still pray?

Jesus

Very little. Don't imitate those who think that because their prayers are long, slow and monotonous, they are excellent. Saying such prayers is more like using a grindstone than a singing lute. Such people set out to pray, but forgetful of their purpose, they are soon lulled to sleep by the rhythm of their repeated phrases, like travellers dozing on their clip-clopping mules.

No, you should pray in secret, and not for long, for it is discourteous to be too insistent. The best prayer is that said most secretly. Pray ... as I have taught Photine to pray.

As he speaks, his hand presses gently on Photine's shoulder to bring her to her knees.

Yes, wherever you live, whether it's Sichem or Jerusalem, when you want to pray do it without ostentation, without pointless cries, without empty chanting, without pressing your head to the ground. No longer should you turn to face Jerusalem or Garizim to please your God, for the Almighty Father is everywhere.

Photine

But close your eyes and pray quietly, almost to yourself, as it is within your own heart above all that he is always there, saying simply: "Our Father in heaven, may your Name be praised; may your kingdom come, and your Will be done on earth as it is in heaven. Give us this day our heavenly bread; forgive our debts as we forgive others their debts to us; do not leave our hearts in danger when tempted, but free us from the Evil One."

The Crowd

Amen!

CURTAIN

The Last Night of Don Juan

(La Dernière Nuit de Don Juan)

Edmond Rostand

A dramatic poem in two parts,
with a prologue

English version by Sonia Yates
& Sue Lloyd

INTRODUCTION

Don Juan chosen as chief protagonist of his last play from the creator of *Cyrano de Bergerac* and *Chantecler*? What is going on here? Has the now middle-aged poet, disillusioned by his experience of life, lost his idealism in making the adulterer par excellence his hero? Not at all. His 'lessons for the soul' have not changed. In his earlier plays, Rostand's heroes have, or learn to have, a creative and positive attitude to life. In *La Dernière Nuit de Don Juan* (*The Final Night of Don Juan*), the poet focuses instead on the destruction caused to human beings and their souls by a cynical, negative attitude to life. The archetypal seducer is presented here without any admiration for his exploits. He is shown to be incapable of true love even when it is offered to him. Lacking any human worth, he will spend eternity as a puppet.

Edmond Rostand was appalled by the fin-de-siècle cynism of his times. He sought to offer instead a positive, passionate attitude to life, imperfect though it is. He believed that, just as the sun lights up banal reality, so idealism and love can transform ordinary life into something creative and wonderful. His heroes: Cyrano, Chantecler, Mélissinde and l'Aiglon, as well as many lesser characters, all have to cope with disillusion and disappointment, but this only strengthens their acceptance of life and enthusiasm for their work.

Don Juan, however, uses his perception that life is imperfect as an excuse to waste his talents and potential, living for solely his own pleasure, seducing women and debasing human love to nothing more than the sexual act. In Rostand's work, such solely physical love is always shown as negative and destructive, a selfish distraction from creativity and duty. Pure love, on the other hand, has a redemptive quality: Roxane in *Cyrano de Bergerac*; the Samaritan woman Photine; Mélissinde in *La Princesse lointaine* and La Faisane in *Chantecler* are all transformed by such love. In *La Dernière Nuit de Don Juan,* the eponymous hero is offered the chance to be redeemed by the pure love of a woman: he does not take it.

La Dernière Nuit de Don Juan contains some wonderfully dramatic moments, poetic beauty and much wit. It was written to be read rather than performed, so it includes some special effects that would be difficult to portray on stage.

The action begins where Molière's play about Don Juan ends, with the statue of the Commander dragging Don Juan down towards hell and

Sganarelle shouting above for his wages. This is the point where other retellings of the legend end. But in the Prologue to Rostand's original and imaginative interpretation, the Don convinces the Devil to give him ten more years of life in which to do the Devil's own work, in his case, seducing women and then abandoning them.

Part One of the play is set in Venice, ten years later. Don Juan, arrogantly revelling in his life of luxury and debauchery, believes the Devil has forgotten about their pact. He is mistaken. The Devil arrives to claim him in the guise of a puppet-master. When Don Juan claims he has no fear of hell or the devil, the little devil puppet makes a contract with him: he will only carry him off to hell if he screams for mercy. With a flourish, the Devil summons the Shades (phantoms of the living or the dead) of the women on Don Juan's list. Don Juan's claim to have 'possessed' every woman he seduced is shown to be hollow.

In Part Two, layer upon layer of the Don's arrogant pride in his own greatness as an antihero is peeled away. Don Juan's abuse of sensual love means that he has never fully developed as a human being, and is now incapable of true love. He will spend eternity as a puppet, manipulated by the puppet master as he was manipulated by his own desires in life.

Origins of the Play

The Don Juan legend has inspired many dramatists of whom the first was Tirso de Molina. His play, entitled *El Burlador de Sevilla y convidado de Piedra* (1630) already contains the main elements found in later interpretations: the seducer ('el burlador'), the wronged women and Don Juan's death after daring to share a meal with a stone statue of a man he has killed, who drags him off to hell. Rostand has his Don Juan singing 'C'est moi le fameux Burlador'; the devil taunts him with knowing his own legend too well.

Molière's *Don Juan et le Festin de Pierre* is naturally the basis as well as the starting point for Rostand's interpretation. We have the stone statue, the Don's servant Sganarelle, the wronged women and even the Poor Man, to whom the Don had given a gold coin 'for the love of humanity' (i.e. not for the love of God). But Rostand took and played with the idea of the list of Don Juan's conquests from Da Ponte's libretto for Mozart's opera *Don Giovanni*: one thousand and three, though in the opera these numbers were his conquests in Spain alone. There are also references to Goethe's version of the Faust legend. This had always fascinated Rostand; he had worked at a verse translation of Part One, on and off, for most of his life.[1] Both Goethe's Mephistopheles and Rostand's Devil embody the idea of negativity and cynicism. And for both poets, true love is selfless, concerned only with the well-being of the beloved.

From Goethe's vision of Faust, Rostand may also have taken the idea that hope, faith and patience are 'fruits that rot before they are picked'. Rostand's image is of a worm in every fruit. Both Faust and Don Juan, lacking faith in the essential goodness of life, make a pact with the devil. But Faust, unlike Don Juan, is finally released from his pact because of his transforming love for Gretchen. In most versions of the legend, Don Juan, too is offered the chance to save his life and soul by a woman's pure love.

Another version of the Don Juan legend which may have contributed to Rostand's vision is *Don Juan Tenorio,* the play by José Zorilla y Moral (known as Zorilla) published in 1844. Rostand almost certainly knew this play; he made several translations from the Spanish of Zorilla's poems as a schoolboy. In Zorilla's play, Don Juan is saved in his last hour by the true love of a nun, Dona Inès. Here an hourglass rather than the flame in a tear of pure love marks the time left for the Don to redeem himself.

The Writing of the Play

After his almost fatal brush with pleurisy in 1900, during the triumphant success of his play for Sarah Bernhardt, *L'Aiglon,* Rostand was advised by his doctor to convalesce in the Basque countryside at Cambo-les-Bains. Here, while he rested his body, his imagination continued to be active. Although he was not allowed for medical reasons to write at first, he began to think about a trilogy, showing Faust, Don Juan and Polichinelle (Punch) as different aspects of the spirit of doubt and negativity which he so deplored.

We can presume that for the first play in the trilogy, Rostand was intending to build on his own incomplete verse translation of Goethe's *Faust, Part One. La Dernière Nuit de Don Juan* was to have been a bridge between *Faust* and *Polichinelle*, where the last scene of *La Dernière Nuit de Don Juan* would be the first scene in the third play in the trilogy. Rostand loved puppet shows and, with his wife Rosemonde, sometimes staged them himself. His vivid boyhood memories of watching Punch and his antics play a large role in *La Dernière Nuit de Don Juan*. But the trilogy idea was put aside when Rostand began work on his next major play, *Chantecler.*

---

[1] This is now available in an edition assembled and edited by Philippe Bulinge: *Faust de Goethe* (éditions THÉATRALES, Montreuil 2007)

Chantecler, first performed in 1910, was a success as far as ticket sales went. But the poet was disturbed by the general failure of audiences to understand the true meaning of his play. He resolved in future to write plays to be read rather than performed. This is why *La Dernière Nuit de Don Juan* is described as 'Poème dramatique' on the title page.

However, when Rostand's good friend, the well-known actor Charles Le Bargy, asked him in 1911 for a play to perform at his last appearance at the Comédie-Française, Rostand thought of building on the fragments of dialogue he had already written for *La Dernière Nuit de Don Juan.* In the event, the play was not finished in time for Le Bargy's farewell; the First World War prevented a planned later performance, and *La Dernière Nuit de Don Juan,* though published by Fasquelle in 1921, did not finally reach the stage until March 1922, more than three years after Rostand's death. Although it was then warmly received, it has not been revived since in France, perhaps because of the problems of staging it in the theatre, as Rostand had foreseen. The few earlier English translations are now out of print.

La Dernière Nuit de Don Juan is as fresh and pertinent today as when Rostand wrote it, and well worthy of being rediscovered by our own cynical and amoral times.

PROLOGUE

Nothing can be seen but a narrow stairway, dimly lit. It spirals upwards out of sight and plunges downwards into an abyss. Splashes of sulphurous green light fall on the lower steps. As the curtain rises, the Statue of the Commander appears, coming down the stairway with a heavy tread. The Statue is holding Don Juan by the arm. Don Juan is magnificently calm.

DON JUAN, THE STATUE OF THE COMMANDER, THE DEVIL (offstage)

Don Juan: Let go of my arm. I'll go down on my own ...

He recites a woman's name at each step.

Ninon, Laure, Agnès, Jeanne ...

A dog can be heard whining. **Don Juan** *listens.*

Ah! Do you hear that? My spaniel, whining for me. A fine creature, Sir.

He continues his descent.

Amanda ... Elvire ...

He stops.

Ah! Permit us to stop a moment, honoured Commander. My faithful valet, who was saying such nice words to me up there, is calling to me. Please let me hear his cry of pain.

Voice of Sganarelle, *above:* My wages!

Don Juan, *to the Statue:* May I retrace my steps for a moment, Sir, to pay him what I owe him?

Statue: You may. I'll wait for you here.

Don Juan: A thousand thanks.

He climbs back up the stairway.

Statue, *alone:* Will he return?

Don Juan, *coming back down the steps*: There, now we're all square. I've given him the kick up the backside that he deserved.

Statue: You've come back then?

Don Juan: Yes, that did me good. I'll fry all the better for it.

Statue: You're not afraid of anything, are you, Don Juan? My old warrior's heart is touched by your courage. Look here, I'll spare you. Go back up again.

Don Juan: You should have said that earlier. As it is, I can feel something grabbing the hem of my coat. A claw has fastened itself into the brocade. It's too late now.

To the enormous claw which has in fact seized the hem of his coat:

Signor Devil, I presume?

A cock crows in the distance.

Statue: Don Juan, day is about to break. That raucous cry means that I must remount my pedestal. Try to pull yourself free of that claw.

The Statue goes back up the steps.

Don Juan: You can be sure I will. But be kind enough to leave the door of the tomb open as you leave.

He pulls gently at his coat.

Now, Claw, let's have a chat. There's really no need to be annoyed because that excellent piece of marble deigned to let me go. Give me another five years on earth. Or even better, ten? There's still much mischief I can do up there. Aha! That has convinced you! After all, let's admit, between ourselves, that I only have a few names on my list so far. Really, Claw, it would be well worth your while to make a pact with me. I'm the one who succeeds best at making people commit the sinful Act — I'm the best hunter in your pack. And besides — come on, do let go of my coat! — there's more to me than there was to that Dr Faust. He only asked for a good little German serving wench. Fool that he was, he was heart-broken when she became pregnant with his child, and called in an angel to defend him at the last!

That marble phantom's fingers have scarred my arm with five scorch marks. How I'd like to show women that tattoo! Just let go of my coat, My Lord, and I'll go far. There's more than one Spanish Infanta sleeping peacefully beneath her pale mosquito net who needs me to disturb her slumbers. As the Corrupter, I'm your deputy. Just let go of me!

The claw releases its grip and withdraws.

About time too! Ten years will be enough. Your Grace can come and find me then. Your Grace can count on me, and for my part, I'm counting on Your Grace.

He re-ascends the stairs, reciting at each step.

Rose ... Lise ... Angélique ... Armande ...

His voice fades as he ascends out of sight. A moment later he can be heard shouting: Hey! Sganarelle! Where are you?

PART ONE

Ten years later. A palace in Venice. A large room looking out over the Adriatic. Marble steps lead down to the water. Centre stage, a table set for a meal, lit by torches.

Scene One

DON JUAN, SGANARELLE

Don Juan: Arabella ... Lucinde ... Isabelle ... Isabeau ...

Sganarelle: The ten years are up, sir.

Don Juan: What fine weather we're having! I've just come back from the Grand Canal.

Sganarelle: Oh yes?

Don Juan: On the rose and amber water, each boat trails a carpet in its wake. The lagoon seems to be holding back the boat by its wake, as Potiphar's wife grasped Joseph's mantle as he fled. But in this quiet corner, the water, more mysteriously green here, slumbers beneath a sky of turquoise and yellow, like some dowdy paragon of virtue before I passed by. I've always been attracted to still water. Do you know why I am so interested in the Adriatic, Sganarelle?

Sganarelle: No.

Don Juan: It's because she's married.

Sganarelle: Really?

Don Juan: She's the wife of the Doge. The Doge is her husband, but I am her lover. I'm the one who really understands you, Lagoon!

Sganarelle: Of course!

Don Juan: So that her waters will dally dissolutely with me, I too will throw her a ring ... from my left hand.

He throws the ring into the lagoon.

Sganarelle, *aghast*: Not the ruby?

Don Juan: No, the glass ring.

Sganarelle: Oh?

Don Juan: Yes.

Sganarelle, *appalled*: Her ring? The one that belonged to ...? So ...

Don Juan: Yes.

Sganarelle: It's over? Stale news? Ancient history?

Don Juan: Ah, Venice! She's the city of all that's fragile: her pillars are stuccoed, her stonework like lace, her walls are mirrors and her streets, water. And when two lovers exchange a ring, Sganarelle, that ring has the wit to be made of glass!

Sganarelle: The ten years are up, but you ...

Don Juan: I carry on as before.

Sganarelle: So this evening ...

Don Juan: I'm off to the ball!

Sganarelle: Are you coming home afterwards?

Don Juan: Not me! I'm stronger than Hannibal! I'm going to take advantage of my victory ... after the ball!

Sganarelle: But sir, if your time is up, all this fine insolence ...?

A clock strikes.

Don Juan: Talk of the time and the clock strikes.

Sganarelle: Oh!

Don Juan: Hush! Let's listen to the peal as it floats away from the campanile.

Sganarelle: Is it worth tarrying so long beneath these skies, sir, just for the pleasure of calling a bell tower a campanile?

Don Juan: I love the white slippers worn by the girls of Venice. I love having a gondolier as a go-between, a gondolier who sings and recites poetry and gets to know you. The ladies of Venice perfume their bath-water with cedar essence. It's enough to put Hippolytus at the mercy of

Phaedra. Venice is a place full of opportunities for me: regattas, balls, processions! I love Venice! Besides, its lion, with a flock of white doves at its feet, is like me. With huge and bitter disdain, this lion renounces its rule over the sea in order to rule over love instead. Yes, crazy but profound city, as I desire to live on my own reflection, I too have built upon the waves!

Sganarelle: This city is deadly.

Don Juan: Even if it were, every adventurer who desires in dying to smash the finest of glasses comes here to end his life. No, I refuse to flee to live beneath a sterner sky. A city of love saw me draw my first breath; a city of love must see my draw my last. Only one epitaph is suitable for Don Juan: 'He was born in Seville and died in Venice'. But I'm only talking like this to scare you! I think the Devil must have forgotten about us.

Sganarelle: Us! What do you mean, us!

Don Juan: You're right, you're not included in this bargain. In fact, you are my heir!

Sganarelle: Oh! Heir to what?

Don Juan: Well, as you've lived so close to me, your merits will carry more weight in the eyes of the nobility, when you tell them 'I used to work for Don Juan'. And as for the ladies ...

Sganarelle: What do you mean?

Don Juan: You needn't fear any difficulties. You'll always find a master ... and mistresses.

Sganarelle: Mistress – es?

Don Juan: Yes, my good fellow. When Don Juan is no longer there, women, adoring his reflection, will sleep with his valet! Now, my excellent accountant, so indignant about the hearts which I've made beat faster, what's the tally? One thousand and ...

Sganarelle: Three. Let's not make it a thousand and four.

Don Juan: I've never felt fresher or on better form! I went to watch the goldsmiths at work in their slum, looking for little boxes to enclose my love letters. This evening I feel as if my heart, like them, were made of red lacquerware, with the flourishes they love to add traced on it in gold.

Let's eat! Everything's made of gold. Like my life, in fact. They gild everything here, even the oyster shells. Who's to say that the Devil still exists, eh, you rascal? He's finished. Tertullian used to say that years ago. I see my life cascading from one love affair to another, as the streams in an Italian garden fall into fountain after fountain. Get my sword and mask ready. The future belongs to me. I'm going to ....

A voice is heard a long way off:

Burattini!

Don Juan: How charming, these old cries of Venice!

Voice, coming nearer: Burattini! Marionettes!

Don Juan: The sound of his voice hangs in the air.

Sganarelle, *going to look out of a window:* It's the puppet-master going past.

Don Juan: Get him to come up.

Sganarelle, *making signs to the puppet-master:* It's the old man from the Quay of Slaves.

Don Juan: Pulcinella! It's him, then? That's it, he's coming in. I shall be able to dine watching Polichinelle, just like Trimalchio sucking a nut as he watched the floppy puppet dancing.

The puppet-master enters, carrying his paraphernalia.

Scene Two

DON JUAN, SGANARELLE, THE PUPPET-MASTER

Puppet-Master, *bowing obsequiously: Burattini ... Li far ballar ...* puppets ... make them dance.

He displays a piece of parchment: Privileggio ...

Sganarelle: Four wooden post, an old sack, an old blind ...

Puppet-Master: *Casteletto.* Permit I set up?

Don Juan: Go ahead. Where are you from?

Puppet-Master, *putting up his little theatre*: From everywhere. I've travelled everywhere. Known writers, artists, many people. In Holland Monsieur Bayle was spectator.

Don Juan: I've travelled myself, like a legend. Your theatre is where I learnt about life and hard knocks. With its pediment, it always looks like a little Greek temple on stilts. Ah! Childhood!

To the puppet-master: Come a little nearer, please.

Talking to himself:

I can see again the puppet-master lifting a corner of that unchanging curtain to hold out his collecting bowl: 'Don't forget Polichinelle, if you please'...

To Sganarelle: Off with you! Leave me alone with Polichinelle.

Exit Sganarelle. The puppet-master goes into the booth from which, one by one, his puppets will appear.

Scene Three

DON JUAN, THE PUPPET-MASTER

The puppet representing Polichinelle (Punch), *rising up in the puppet theatre*:

Ron — tout — tout! ... Ron — tout — tout!

Don Juan: Ah! That's him! There he is!

Punch Puppet: It's me *Pul!* It's me *chi!* It's me *nella!* It's me again! It's me bumping my nose against the wings!

Don Juan: Ah! This is the kind of theatre I've always loved! Why are you banging your nose like that?

Punch Puppet: Why does anyone bang their nose like that? I'm talking through my nose to sound like a reed flute. I'm banging loudly to imitate the drums of martial glory and I'm singing a tune they taught me in France at the fair.

He sings:

> I am the famous Mignolet,
>
> General of the Spaniolets,
>
> Who sets a-tremble women's hearts!

Don Juan, *raising his glass and singing*:

> I am the famous Burlador,
>
> Who woos the women better for
>
> He wins their hearts with skilful arts!

He breaks off and says to the Punch Puppet: I too can make verses!

Punch Puppet: Well-turned ones too.

Don Juan: Let me tell you, beautiful verses, like beautiful girls, are always permitted to let their finer points show.

Punch Puppet: What you say always has a whiff of the flesh, Don Juan!

Don Juan: You know my name?

Punch Puppet: Yes, colleague.

Don Juan, *rather taken aback:* My dear fellow, in what way am I your colleague?

Punch Puppet: In debauchery!

Don Juan, *imitating him*: In debauchery? You always say the words that shouldn't be said, Polichinelle.

Punch Puppet: My face is redder than yours, and you are more conceited than me, but we shall be equals on the Day of Judgement!

Don Juan: Funny fellow!

The Punch puppet rings a bell.

Why are you ringing that bell?

Punch Puppet: To mark the solemn hour which brings Don Juan and Polichinelle face to face.

Don Juan: So you're calling me a ...

Punch Puppet: For politeness sake, let's not say Polichinelle, but Polygamist.

Don Juan: And to be really precise, let's say 'nulligamist'. Now, bring back my childhood by singing through your nose!

Punch Puppet: Doh, ray, me, fa, sol ...

Don Juan, *remembering:* I'm seeing again in my mind's eye a pale-faced little boy wearing a big collar. He's pale because he's watching the puppet show sitting beside ...

Punch Puppet: Beside whom?

Don Juan: Beside girls whose laughter excused all your peccadilloes.

Punch Puppet: Doh, ray, me ...

Puppet of Cassandra, *appearing in the booth:* You took my daughter away from me, you seducer!

Punch Puppet: You're a nuisance!

He kills her.

Don Juan: Just like me and the Commander!

Punch Puppet: I love Charlotte.

Puppet of Pierrot, *appearing in the booth:* She's mine!

Punch Puppet: What a nuisance he is!

He kills him.

A man has to do what a man has to do!

Dog, *appearing in the booth and leaping on Punch's head:* Woof!

Punch Puppet: That dog's doing what a dog has to do; he's eating my nose!

Don Juan: How they laughed at all the blows that fell on the gullible Pierrots and the honest Cassandras!

Punch Puppet: Who laughed?

Don Juan: The young girls. I was sitting there amongst their skirts. Their beauty amazed me.

Punch Puppet: Could you see their legs?

Don Juan: Hush!

Punch Puppet: As for beauty, for me, you know ... I knew the philosopher Bayle in Rotterdam. This man Bayle was not convinced that even Helen had been beautiful.

Don Juan: What a pedantic prig! To question the beauty of Helen! Dirty-minded prig! The one thing in the world I'm still sure about! Helen! Helen! Tell me where she is, so that I can set off ...

A doll appears in the booth. Don Juan utters a cry: Oh!

Punch Puppet: Back already from your trip to Sparta?

Don Juan: Alas! Beneath the grey skies of this stifling century, the great Helen is dead!

Considering the doll admiringly: Oh! The pretty child! What is this radiant star doing on this humble stage?

Punch Puppet: So, it only takes a piece of wood and some blond hair to console him for the loss of Helen? You see how alike we are, Signor!

To the doll: I love you!

Don Juan: But we don't have quite the same approach.

Punch Puppet, *to Don Juan*: Pardon?

Don Juan: If you say 'I love you', you've lost her.

Punch Puppet: How should I go about it then?

Don Juan: Not too fast, not too slow. Come on, seduce her.

Punch Puppet: But how?

Don Juan: It's an art.

Punch Puppet: Fancy footwork?

Don Juan: Don't be silly.

Punch Puppet: Or with my eyes?

Don Juan: Sheep's eyes?

Punch Puppet: How should I look, then?

Don Juan: As if you're about to engulf her in fathomless depths.

Punch Puppet: That's a bit steep!

Don Juan: She's waiting. She senses that you're going to possess her. You've got her. Now you look the other way.

Punch Puppet: Ah yes! Like this?

Don Juan: An intimidating silence, that's my method. Deceive without telling lies, like the horizon.

Punch Puppet: Soft focus!

Don Juan: And the woman is hooked. Ah! Savour that moment when the line trembles as the bait is taken. For eating the fish is never as good as the struggle to land it!

Punch Puppet: I'm not getting anywhere.

Don Juan: So what are you going to do now?

Punch Puppet: Supposing I got her to read an improper book?

Don Juan: What, win her thanks to Bocaccio or Straparole? I should hate that!

Punch Puppet, *to the doll*: Charlotte, speak to me? No?

He hits her. Whack!

Don Juan: We still have a different approach. You don't hit a woman. You make her suffer.

The Doll Puppet, *interested, to Don Juan*: Really? How?

Punch Puppet, *to Don Juan*: Are you trying to make up to my doll?

He hits her again.

She's an honest woman! She's an honest woman!

Don Juan: She's a dead woman.

Punch Puppet: That's just what I was saying.

He throws the body of the doll up in the air: Up you go!

Don Juan: So now, the Devil's coming?

Punch Puppet: No, it's the watchman next.

Don Juan: Let's skip that scene.

Punch Puppet: Cut that admirable scene? So be it. The judge, then.

Don Juan: Skip it.

Punch Puppet: That scene where I hit him? So be it. The executioner ...

Don Juan: Skip it.

Punch Puppet: Oh well, if we're going to cut everything!

Don Juan: A masterpiece can be adapted to suit oneself and the occasion. And this evening, we can do without the extras. I should like to see someone being carried off by the devil.

Punch Puppet: This evening?

He shakes his little bell.

Don Juan: What o'clock are you ringing?

Punch Puppet: The hour of the werewolf!

He trembles.

I'm frightened ... I sense that he's coming ... he's on his way ...

Don Juan: Where's he coming from? From behind ... Why are you looking round?

The puppet of the Devil appears in the puppet booth.

Devil Puppet: Grrr!

Punch Puppet, *hitting the Devil puppet*: Whack! – Oh no, my stick's broken! Horrid creature!

The Devil puppet has disappeared.

Don Juan: Have you got another stick?

Devil Puppet, *reappearing*: Grrr!

Punch Puppet, *hitting him again*: Whack! I don't believe it!

The Devil puppet has disappeared again.

Don Juan: You don't beat the Devil.

Punch Puppet: You make him suffer?

Don Juan: Yes.

Devil Puppet, *reappearing*: Really? How?

Don Juan: You'll find out when you're a big devil.

Devil Puppet: Drat!

Punch Puppet, *hitting the little Devil puppet with all his might*: Whack! Another stick! ... Whack! Another one ... Whack!

Don Juan: Calm down!

Punch Puppet: Well, I'm frightened.

Don Juan: 'Without fear or remorse', to adapt the knight Bayard's famous motto to suit myself ...

Devil Puppet: One must live one's life ...

Don Juan: And die one's death!

Punch Puppet: He's carrying me off! What's the use of being brave? I'm wailing!

Don Juan, *to the little Devil Puppet*: So you're carrying him off just like that, over your shoulder?

Devil Puppet: Scary, isn't it?

Don Juan: It's interesting. But what a poor show he's putting up.

Devil Puppet: So you'd do better, would you?

Don Juan: Yes.

Devil Puppet: You'd make me suffer?

Don Juan: Yes. Does that upset you?

Devil puppet, *suddenly changing his voice*: I'm intrigued. I'll put my corpse down for a moment. I'd really like to know, my dear fellow, by what means ...

Don Juan: Goodness! That's made you lose your Italian accent?

Devil Puppet: ... you would make me suffer?

Don Juan: You know full well that you suffer if you dangle someone over your bottomless pit and he doesn't turn pale. When you carry people off, you want to have to drag them off by their hair, resisting all the time and grabbing at any handhold. You're only happy if your horns toss them

exhausted and desperate into the fires you fan with your goatish breath!
... Now as for me, if you had carried me off, you would not have had me.

Devil Puppet: Not had you? I like that 'not have had'!

Don Juan: To have had me, my good fellow, you'd have had to drag me off raging mad and howling like this buffoon. Or lying with my eyes closed, pale, breathless ... like the women I used to have. But on my feet, no one has me. Standing at the gateway where Dante engraved his terrifying phrase, I laugh. He did not write it there for me, for I have memories that burn more fiercely than your fangs. You see, me, I am myself!

Devil Puppet: Meaning?

Don Juan: I am a hero! I'm a son of the Conquistadors, woman is my Florida. I am as brave as they were, but more rapacious: I've always wanted to see, from the Indies where I am, the Indies I shall visit next. Anyone who thinks I will repent on my deathbed hasn't seen me when I'm leaving a boudoir. I am the monster with a soul, a savage Archangel who has kept his fallen angel's wings. If, as I pass by, a breath agitates a veil, it's because I haven't been a Polichinelle, his wings coffined in his hump back!

Devil Puppet: So, you're not frightened?

Don Juan: Not of you or any of your kind.

Devil Puppet: What about the flames?

Don Juan: I'll provide them myself.

Devil Puppet: And the horns?

Don Juan: I have some already. I understand that the bravest men may be frightened. Even Marshal Trevulce, faced with a satanic imp as he died, was convulsed with terror. But as for me, I've only ever trembled with desire.

Devil Puppet: As for you, you will beg me not to take you away! I shall only carry you off once you're beaten!

Don Juan: Make a note of that: I am saved!

Devil Puppet, *holding out his little hand from inside the booth*: Let's shake on that!

Don Juan: It's a deal! My hand in your little paw.

Devil Puppet: And mine in yours.

The Devil Puppet disappears.

Don Juan: Whatever am I doing? I've drunk very little sherry, and yet, just when the bewitching hour of the ball is drawing near, I let myself ...

A bell is heard ringing inside the booth.

Why is he ringing that bell? How is it that...

A lantern is extinguished over the sea.

And that lantern, why has it just gone out? ... How is it that I've let myself go so far as to tell that puppet what I've never told a soul before? Come on, Don Juan! You've only wasted a few words. And the time is ...

At that moment the Puppet-Master comes out of the booth. But he's thrown off his Puppet-Master's costume, which was only a disguise. It is the Devil himself.

Oh, it was you! Now I understand why I said those things!

Scene Four

DON JUAN, THE DEVIL

Devil: Don't forget Polichinelle, if you please?

Don Juan: What do you want me to put into your collecting bowl this evening?

Devil: Your soul!

Don Juan: Farewell then, my soul, *donna mobile,* fickle lady!

Devil: Yes, signor, I'm the old puppet-master, the old puppet-master. I'm carrying off in my bag right now a judge, an emperor and three beggars. Also, taking advantage of their apoplexies, I made off with two senators from under the dome of the Procurator's palace. Are you coming into my bag?

Don Juan: I can walk on my own two feet, thank you.

Devil: Yes, I'm the old puppet-master, signor! Off to hell with you!

Don Juan: You've not handled that very well, naively coming here now, talking of hell. You would have caused me much more anguish if you had waited until I was old to fetch me. Old age is the only hell to make me tremble.

Devil: Oh no, I know you! You would never have grown old.

Don Juan: How about taking off those panther-claw gloves of yours and having supper with me, since this is the last evening of my life?

Devil: Yes, your delightful bachelor life. I see two armchairs, upholstered in velvet.

Don Juan: As always.

Devil: And a table laid for two.

Don Juan: As always. I'm always expecting the Devil to supper — or Cleopatra might turn up ... If it's the queen of Egypt, fine! If it's the Devil, too bad!

Music is heard.

My little band of musicians, distantly playing ...

Devil: As always?

Don Juan: As always. Rather nice, isn't it?

Devil: Let's go!

Don Juan: I'll fetch my coat. What do you think of it?

Devil: It's superb!

Don Juan: You have to look the part. Very important, all that kind of thing. We're off then? Do look at the sleeves! Rather better cut than one of M. Dimanche's, don't you think? Where is your gondola?

He calls out: Gondolier Charon! *To the devil*: It's still Charon, I hope?

Devil: What a swaggerer you are, Don Juan!

Don Juan: Oh yes, I'm a great swaggerer.

Devil: I suppose the fair sex expected it?

Don Juan: Are we off!

Devil: Not yet.

Don Juan: You're annoyed I'm not taking this seriously, aren't you?

Devil: Let's eat.

They both sit down at the table.

Don Juan: Are you hoping the wine will make me depressed?

Devil: We'll see.

Don Juan: Dry or sweet?

Devil: Dry!

Don Juan: How do you like the way the table is laid, with the roses? It's part of my job to get these things right, you know.

Devil: So that's very important too?

Don Juan: Of course the setting matters! The furniture is by Brustolon — you can't get better than that!

Devil: Even the furniture?

Don Juan: Yes, you don't want poor taste to spoil Cythera, the home of Venus.

Devil: So you're an interior designer?

Don Juan: Only for rooms designed to assist seduction. How do you like the menu?

Devil: You're a chef?

Don Juan: Well, who would deny the importance of a savoury sauce and fine stuffing for the Romagna hare and the Lombardy quails? You have to be able to cook for yourself to arouse desire, and you must surround yourself with art and literature, too. Women are not as stupid as people think. They are very discriminating and they know they will have a better time with a ...

Devil: Designer, conductor, tailor, chef ...?

Don Juan: Absolutely! It's only right that a lapse from virtue should tease, intrigue and scintillate! Why are you in black, by the way? You don't need to be and it's rather stupid.

Devil: Really?

Don Juan: What did that to you?

Devil: The inkwell Martin Luther threw at my head!

Don Juan: I liked you better in green.

Devil: You saw me?

Don Juan: In Eden! With Eve!

Devil: You saw ...?

Don Juan: I was Adam!

Devil: You remember it?

Don Juan: In dreams. I seem to see us again, beneath the gnarled apple tree. What is this great secret that we learnt then? No one has ever spoken of it ... I was the first man. I was biting into the apple... and I saw wriggling inside it, white and supple, as you were green and supple in the tree, your horrid miniature self ...

Devil: The worm?

Don Juan: I spit it out! Then you say, 'You must try another apple'. So I take a bite from another, but I see the same worm wriggling there. I spit it out. But you say, 'Bite into the others'. I bite: a worm; I bite: a worm; I bite: a worm! 'Every beautiful fruit', you tell us, 'is nothing but a worm in hiding. This is the great secret that no one must know. Now try to live with that knowledge!'

Devil: Try!

Don Juan: We did try. And Eve and I succeeded straight away. The foliage women have used to conceal themselves ever since — their clothes — gave us every permission for vice. And we soon found a way of forgetting for an instant that every good thing conceals a worm.

Devil: And so you became Don Juan.

Don Juan: And so I became the hero who takes his revenge, shouting out as I leave Paradise: 'Yes, raise your sword, Archangel, to guard the garden of your generous master, who makes us a gift of a tree with fruits ridden with worms. As for me, I relinquish any claim to it. Joyfully abandoning Jacob's ladder for a silken ladder, I mock this Paradise that you reserve for the pure, because, for one Paradise lost, a thousand are regained!'

Devil: One thousand and three! — I don't much care for explanations with a whiff of Ecclesiastes!

Don Juan: Yes, since all is vanity, and everything is worth nothing ...

Devil: Let's try to make a nothing worth everything!

Don Juan: I discovered how to create a fruit with the most wonderful taste!

Devil: But what about heaven, then?

Don Juan: When I take hold of someone's face, I make a miniature heaven for myself in her eyes.

Devil: And truth?

Don Juan: Rising from the depths of her frills and furbelows, it's Woman!

Devil: And glory?

Don Juan: There's only one worth having, the Victory that literally comes to us undoing her sandal!

Devil, *getting up and putting his hand on Don Juan's shoulder:* So I am carrying you off like this, thrilled to have been ...?

Don Juan, *also rising:* The only hero that people truly admire! Just read their books! Watch their plays! Everything bears me out. With what a glistening eye virtue detests me! What do so many dull and plodding men expect from becoming powerful, but that they can believe for one instant that they are me? With what passion and envy scholars delve into the smallest details of my life! What man does not secretly admire me for daring the embrace which he felt too ugly or too cowardly to dare himself? For all of them, I'm the one who took the opportunities they wistfully regret not taking. For all your hissing, you old serpent, there's no work, no virtue, no knowledge and no belief that is not really the regret of not having been Don Juan!

Devil: And what will remain of all this to you now?

Don Juan: The same as remained to Alexander: his ashes know that they were once Alexander. But because I was myself my own army, I possessed all this personally, all by myself!

Devil: You possessed? Possess, that's the word they use. But my dear champion of immorality, what, after all, have you possessed?

Don Juan, *calling out:* Sganarelle!

Scene Five

DON JUAN, THE DEVIL, SGANARELLE

Don Juan, *to Sganarelle who has come in*: My list!

Sganarelle, *terrified at seeing the Devil*: Oh!

Don Juan: Yes. Take the ruby ring and go.

Sganarelle, *to the Devil*: *Vade retro*! Get thee behind me, Satan!

To Don Juan, giving him the list: Do I have to read it out to ...?

Don Juan: No. There are too many names on it.

Sganarelle exits.

Scene Six

DON JUAN, THE DEVIL

Devil: You leave no one? Not one son?

Don Juan: It wasn't worth the trouble. It was that drunkard Silene's son Staphylus who first adulterated wine with water, you know. Would I let a son water down my wine? No, thank you! This is the end. Finis! Good night! Shall we go?

Devil: Not yet. It's that word 'possess' that you use ... Of course, I know what it means for me to possess someone – people talk about someone being 'possessed' by the Devil, but for a human being to possess anyone? Possess? Can we try to pin down the active rather than passive meaning of that verb?

Don Juan: You satyr! I can see your yellow eye shining with obscene thoughts!

Devil: I'm just dipping my toe into the bowl of significant words ...

Don Juan: Your goat's hoof, you mean!

Devil: 'Then they went to bed', it says in books. Is that what 'to possess' means? Nothing more terrible than that?

Don Juan: 'Then he knew her', it says in the Bible. To possess someone is to know her, to know her as a person and to know her as a fact. You can see clearly how terrible that is.

Devil: So you have to have known her in order to ...

Don Juan: Possess her!

Devil: And you did 'know' them?

Don Juan: I have clasped their naked souls to my bosom. No one understood their game better than I. That gallant, the duc de Richelieu, and his like? Children aping me! No one else saw through them as I did, causing them to crumple up so many little handkerchiefs in fits of temper! I could tear up my list!

Devil: That's right, let's tear it up!

Don Juan: I know all their names!

Devil: Let's tear it up!

Don Juan: I know the name, the day, the reason, the lie! All their secrets are there! I dip my hand distractedly into all these memories of a certain evening or morning like a pensive conqueror toying with his booty. I'll tell you some of these stories if you like. To conjure up a complete person, all it needs is for me to chew over a name, as if I were sucking on a flower.

Devil: Let's put all these pieces of your heart into your hat!

Don Juan: Not one of them was a woman of easy virtue, you know.

Devil: Let's tear it up! We need to tear the list into one thousand and three pieces ...

Don Juan: I liked to be able to sense their remorse.

Devil: Let's tear it up!

Don Juan: Just as lions don't touch dead bodies, I kept away from flesh which had lost its soul. Oh look, between us we are tearing apart all of woman, body and soul!

Devil: I see you were loved by the whole alphabet, from A to Z ...

Don Juan: I've got the Z here: Zulma. There's still some Bs left: the four Brigittes. It's done.

Devil: And now ...

With a conjuror's flourish, he suddenly makes a small violin appear.

Don Juan: You do magic tricks?

Devil: I always keep a small violin in my pocket. The old puppet-master is a dancing master too ... *La la la* ... who can even make fallen leaves whirl ... Sing, my violin, violin that the devil goes about playing at night, violin made of the wood of which beloved women are made, sing under the bow made of the wood which makes Don Juans!

As he plays, he is talking to the scraps of paper, which begin to quiver mysteriously in Don Juan's hat.

Dance, little fragments of an intoxicated life! Dance a gavotte! ...

Don Juan: What are you doing, dancing around like a madman?

Devil: This is the Gavotte of the Torn-up List ... aroused by your names, rise out of the hat and flutter on the floor!

Don Juan, *gazing at the fragments of his list as they rise swirling into the air:* Where are they going? Where are they going?

Devil: I think they want to fly away! Aha! If you fly away, little butterflies each formed from a life, then fly away white, white, over the lagoon! Off you go!

The fragments have whirled far away in a column and then separated to fall like snow onto the water.

Now a lively farandole ... and suddenly, on the silken water, breeze-rippled, all these sweet fragments bearing charming names grow and grow, lengthening into black silhouettes and becoming slowly gliding gondolas.

At this moment, gondolas appear far off on the lagoon.

Don Juan: What is this strange little fleet?

Devil: Now for a barcarolle! Each of your love affairs was like a trip in a gondola: sweet encouragement, an embrace, and then a bereavement as you departed. See them glide along, each one a gently-rocking boat, an alcove and a coffin!

Don Juan: How swiftly my loves glide along in the moonlight!

Devil: See how they mingle, long, dark and narrow ...

Don Juan: Yet more gondolas!

Devil: Now there are one thousand and one! One thousand and two! One thousand and three!

To the gondolas, now already nearing the terrace: Come closer! Come closer!

Don Juan: Each one is like a wandering star!

Devil: And all are guided by my hand alone! Would you like this one with the emerald lantern to draw up to the foot of steps and allow its phantom to land?

Don Juan, *with a start*: What did you say?

Devil: Or shall I hail this one with the lantern of amethyst?

Don Juan: These marvellous gondolas are not empty, then?

Devil: No. As each gondola is a name on your list, it contains the shade of a woman which has blossomed from her name. They are all there, all one thousand and three! I, more powerful than Paracelsus, I have given them a double life if they are still alive, or awoken them from the dead. So which woman would you like to see arise from the black cushions and place her golden slipper on the quay?

Don Juan: Several!

Devil: *leaning out over the water and calling out*: Quick now! Disembark!

Don Juan, *taking the gilt candlestick and going to stand, motionless, at the top of the steps:* The shades are coming up!

One by one the women emerge out of the shadows at the top of the steps.

Devil: All masked by the great white mask of Venice!

Don Juan: White slippers, come and crush the herbs strewn on the marble!

He puts down the candlestick and throws himself into an armchair.

Devil, *capering around playing his violin:* Come on now, step ashore!

A Shade: Good evening, Don Juan!

Devil: Come on! Step ashore!

Women, all alike, clad in a long cloak, white mask and holding a fan, continue to appear at the top of the steps.

Don Juan: It's like the landing on Venus's island of Cythera!

Devil, *coming back towards Don Juan, but continuing to play*: Yes, but painted by the disturbing Longhi, not by the gentle Watteau. Watteau isn't around any more when people disembark ...

Don Juan: Silvery-blue shades are coming up the steps from the water!

Devil: Each exactly like the other, and combining in their frail attire the essentials of a love affair: the cloak, the mask, the fan and the rose ...

Don Juan: The rose, the cloak, the mask and the fan !

The stage is now full of shades, who continue to disembark.

Scene Seven

DON JUAN, THE DEVIL, THE 1003 SHADES

All the Shades: Good evening, Don Juan!

Don Juan, *gallantly, to the Shades:*

May I offer you something? An ice, perhaps? A delicious fruit? Or the lightest of cakes? And, while leaving you your fans and roses, may I remove your masks and cloaks?

Devil, *smartly, and tapping the violin briskly with his bow*: No!

Don Juan gets out of his chair, looking with surprise at the Devil.

Devil, *speaking more gently and bowing to Don Juan:*

But each one, still wrapped in her cloak, and with her face concealed by her fan, will, in just three words, paint the portrait of her soul for you as she plucks the petals from her rose. And if you say her name, her mask will fall!

A Shade: Try me ...

She whispers into Don Juan's ear.

Don Juan: So quietly?

Devil: Unless you can find a woman who can tell her story out loud!

Don Juan, *stroking the Shade's hand*: You ...

Devil: Nothing but the soul! No touching the flesh!

Don Juan, *to the Shade:* Every time, a pang of remorse afterwards? You always were virtuous after the event, Lucile!

A Shade: What a charmer!

Don Juan: There, you see! It's easy!

A Shade: Just the way he says 'Lucile'!

Don Juan: Yes, I'll say it again, Lucile ...

The First Shade: Almost you persuade me that I am she ...

Don Juan: What?

The First Shade: No!

Don Juan: But ...

Another Shade: And me?

Don Juan: You ...

Again he goes to take hold of the Shade's hand.

Devil, *rapping his bow across Don Juan's fingers*: No touching the flesh!

Don Juan: Oh, I know your name! You ... you ... you ... How could I make a mistake? You ... yes, it was you ... there were fireworks that evening ... we lost your mother and her dog in the crowd ...

The Same Shade: yes, I was a bit unsteady in the crush ...

Don Juan: But I soon steadied you, Suzanne!

The Same Shade: No!

Don Juan: What? But those details ...

Devil: Superficial.

Don Juan: It's true that in my life there have been so many mothers, so many dogs and so many firework displays ...!

Another Shade: And me?

Don Juan: You ... you ... you ... you ... What? Rather disappointed? Well it's hard to make love well on a summit, your so Serene Highness!

The Same Shade: No!

Another Shade: And me?

Don Juan: You ... Bellagio ... the Villa des Anthèmes ... Miss Ethel ...

The Same Shade: No!

Don Juan: What?

Devil: No more Ethel ... than Miss!

Don Juan: Wait a moment ... What is this flood of nostalgia invading my heart? Oh yes, it's the daughter of my school caretaker!

The Same Shade: No!

Another Shade: And me?

Don Juan: This heart bursting like an overblown carnation ... Ah yes, it's my little bull-fight evening with you, Conchita!

The Same Shade: No!

Another Shade: And me?

Don Juan: Ah, now this time ...

Devil: Who is it?

Don Juan: My aunt, who was so jealous of my niece!

The Same Shade: No!

Don Juan: I don't believe it!

He listens to another Shade:

Ah, you! ... That word gives you away: unmask your Russian nose, Princess Olga!

The Same Shade: No!

Don Juan: What?

Another Shade: And me?

Don Juan: Lucy ... you were the clever one who had read Brantôme ...

The Same Shade: No!

Don Juan, *pushing her away*: Oh!

Devil: Don't you damage any of my phantoms!

Don Juan: They are deceiving me!

Devil: They are telling you the truth.

Don Juan, *with an ear to another Shade:* Well?

To the Devil: She's not telling me anything!

Devil: That's because there was nothing to tell!

Don Juan: Lucy ... Anne ... Emma ...Zoé ... Berthe ... Emmeline ...

Devil: Search!

Another Shade: Me?

Don Juan: You? He's got his back to us ... give me something to go on! Take off your mask!

The Shade takes off her mask, only to reveal another mask.

Don Juan: Another mask?

Without dropping her disguise, the Shade takes off several masks one after the other.

Don Juan: Another mask? Another? Yet another? Do they go on for ever?

Devil: For ever. She's one of those women who only have layers of masks instead of a face.

Don Juan: But I'm not tipsy! The wine has stayed in the bottle. I'm afraid of all these eyes looking straight at me! I do have a right to see the eyes, they are not made of flesh. It's the eyes that will enlighten me! Why has it suddenly got much darker? Now they are not enigmatic any more.

Devil: Is that a problem?

Don Juan: It makes it difficult for me to recognise them.

Devil: Yes indeed! Without the skin, without the hair, and sometimes, even without the hat!

Don Juan: I don't recognise these Bacchante-like stares!

Devil: Perhaps you didn't meet too many Bacchantes!

Don Juan: It's as if I'm seeing them for the first time, these big, simple eyes!

Devil: It's because this evening, they are looking straight at you with the eyes of their ancestors, the eyes they had when you were not there!

Don Juan: You're lying!

The Shades, *laughing*: Ha ha ha ha!

Don Juan: Oh yes, go on, laugh, laugh! I knew you would end up by betraying yourselves. It's possible to recognise your heaving bosoms when you laugh, and you might say ... But what is this strange laughter they have tonight?

Devil: It's the laugh they might have shared together sometimes, a laugh no man has ever heard.

Don Juan: No, I knew it.

Devil: Ah! Human beings! Human beings! Does anyone really know them? Can anyone ever know them?

Don Juan: He can caper around like a monkey all he likes, I shall recognise them ... I shall carry round the candlestick ...

A Shade, *laughing*: Ha ha!

Don Juan: That wickedly bizarre laugh over there ... It's Archangela Tarabotti, the girl from Monaco!

The Shade: No!

New Shades are arriving all the time.

Don Juan: They're still coming!

Devil: Come ashore!

Don Juan: Heaven and earth! I certainly knew at least one of these creatures! Come on, let me see your eyes! I'm telling you to let me see your eyes! No more laughing! Elvira must be here somewhere. I did know her, Elvira!

Devil: Keep searching, then!

Don Juan: I shall take the tall gilt candelabra ...

He seizes it.

Devil: Search!

Don Juan: And all night, if necessary, I shall hold the light to your faces, and peer into those twin abysses which conceal your deepest selves!

Devil: Sing, little violin ...

Don Juan: Oh!

Devil: Why these angry outbursts? Keep on looking!

Don Juan: Yes, the whole night ... Keep calm! My mistakes don't count. I'm beginning in earnest now. These dramatic eyes ... Olga?

The Shade: No!

Don Juan, *speaking to another Shade:* These romantic eyes ... Lucy?

The Shade: No!

Don Juan: Keep calm! ... Shall I start again? These eyes here ... Keep calm ... it's ... it's ...

And Don Juan, going from Shade to Shade, carries on his search. The curtain slowly falls.

PART TWO

The scene is as before. Day is beginning to break. Don Juan, moving through the crowd of Shades, is still searching and still trying out names.

Scene One

DON JUAN, THE DEVIL, THE THOUSAND AND THREE SHADES; later, THE WHITE SHADE

Don Juan: ... ...

Devil: Will daybreak find you still seeking the Woman, with your purple cloak and glowing lamp, as Diogenes sought for an honest man?

Don Juan: Oh!

He throws aside the candelabra.

And to think I have tasted sleep in all these arms!

Devil: Yes ...

Don Juan: All night I've been trying out names! ... I've been wandering from one stranger ...

He tries one last time: Lucile?

A Shade: No!

Don Juan: ... to another stranger! I can hear all these names whirling around my head like a fearsome flock of birds! And not one knows where to land. And yet we did make love together, didn't we?

The Shades: We did!

Don Juan: I am alone in a forest of souls. They are all there. Yet I have searched and searched. All my life I have always abandoned friendship, where one might get to know another person, for the love in which two people cannot know each other. So I shall die without having known a single other being!

Devil: You've seen nothing! You've known nothing! You've had nothing!

A Shade: Like a fisherman who desires a pearl but never dives for it, you've only possessed what can be possessed quickly ...

Don Juan: It's all lies!

Another Shade: Since when did you want the truth? As soon as a Man has spoken his first word, Woman knows which lie to offer him.

Another Shade: You wanted me an intellectual, so I spoke of Petrarch.

Another Shade: Since your desire at that moment was for someone exotic, I affected an air of mystery which was no mystery to me.

Another Shade: Seeing that you fancied an impudent woman from the provinces, I pursed my lips into a pout.

Another Shade: Sensing that you needed your happiness blighted, I smiled at my husband in your presence one evening.

Another Shade: Ever since men created the Agneses and the Omphales, being a woman has consisted of serving up to them, when desire has dulled their wits, men's own invention, the eternal Feminine!

Devil: So all you have done is keep company with some conundrums ... and now I can carry you off!

Don Juan: Get your claws off me! My ancestors were no less the conquerors of the Indies because the Indians themselves remained a mystery.

Devil: So, possession?

Don Juan: Possession is domination. My prodigious energy has satisfied that spirit which theology calls the spirit of ... of ...

Devil: Principality.

Don Juan: I have dominated! This cannot be denied. I'm a prince who combines the unscrupulousness of Macchiavelli with the insolence of Aretino.

Devil: What it is to have travelled in Italy! My fine little Andalusian, so sensual and thoughtless! You thought you were travelling, but you simply took on board whatever each nation adds to lust!

Don Juan: I have been a corruptor!

Devil: So that's your surest claim to glory?

To the Shades:

When were you first aware of having the desire to sin?

The Shades: The first day! — The first evening! — On seeing you! — I'd already thought about it before I saw you. — It was after I had already chosen you that you looked at me.

Don Juan: There were some virgins.

Devil: Yes that's what they call the ones who choose you with their eyes cast down.

Don Juan, *leaping towards the Shades*: But I did seduce you!

A Shade: Once we had made up your mind for you!

Don Juan: How?

Another Shade: By the sign.

Several Shades: Yes, by giving you the sign.

Don Juan: There were some fine ladies ...

Another Shade: Those are the ones who make the smallest gesture!

Don Juan: But ...

The Shades: Try to remember: everything! — Nothing! — A perfume lingered over! — A flower pulled apart ... — a child kissed ... — a laugh that dies away ...

Devil: — A silence in which I pass by ...

Don Juan: So?

The Shades: Remember!

Don Juan: No, no! it's not true! You're lying!

A Shade: You grandly dictated to us our own desires.

Don Juan: There were Cinderellas in headlong flight ...

A Shade: But always careful to leave a slipper behind!

Another Shade: The silken ladders by which you climbed to our chambers, Don Juan, weren't they rather spiders' webs?

Don Juan: *with a bitter laugh*: So I've spent my life ...

Devil: Believing that you made your own way into hearts where I was already waiting for you ...

Don Juan: So seducing you?

Devil: 'Oh, how I've seduced the magnet!', as iron says to itself.

Another Shade: You are simply the one we most offered to ourselves!

Another Shade: The one we passed round laughing to one another!

Another Shade: Where is he now? Like 'pass the parcel'!

Don Juan: I thought I was the wicked wolf in the wild forest, but I was only the ferret of Bois-Joli in the rhyme.

All the Shades, *singing in a circle round Don Juan*:

> He runs, he runs, the ferret,
>
> The ferret of the woods, ladies!
>
> He runs, he runs, the ferret,
>
> The ferret of Bois-Joli!

Devil: *tapping the heart of a Shade with his bow*: He went this way!

Tapping on another heart: He'll come back that way!

And suddenly throwing himself onto Don Juan: And now I'm carrying you off, duped, humiliated, your pride in tatters ...

Don Juan: *freeing himself*: Not yet!

Devil, *drawing back and looking at him*: You still have something to be proud of?

Don Juan, *leaning back against the high back of a chair, with his arms crossed*: I still have ...

Devil: You want to try again?

Don Juan: You want to prevent me?

He totters, wipes his hand over his perspiring brow and mutters to himself: Now I face my greatest duel.

Devil: And your last! What new source of pride have you found?

Don Juan: The pride of iron!

Devil: Iron that is filed down!

Don Juan: Iron that feels that, because it is preferred by the magnet to all other metals, it must have some special virtue!

Devil, *gentle again*: So what remains to you is that you have pleased women?

Don Juan: Enormously! How could you think that a man could give way to doubt, when he knows his own deep worth from the vertiginous thrill he gives to women? To please is a man's greatest gift.

Devil: Who says so? Being disdained by a foolish woman was the making of Spinoza, and it was his broken nose that made a great artist of Michelangelo!

Don Juan: Giving pleasure is the greatest sign, and the strangest.

Devil: Ask them why you pleased them ...

Don Juan, *to a Shade*: You?

The Shade, *coming forward with a little laugh*: Me?

Don Juan, *suddenly*: No! Perhaps it's better not to know why!

Devil, *with his hand already on Don Juan's shoulder*: Aha, are you trembling?

Don Juan, *to the Shade*: Speak.

The Shade: Because you gave off a certain scent...

Don Juan: The scent of the abyss?

The Shade: The scent of mild tobacco, boudoirs and the fencing hall.

Another Shade: You pleased us for the same reasons that made you displeasing to other men.

Another Shade: Because women are your profession.

Another Shade: Because you are the one we blush most about.

Another Shade: Because you give us your undivided attention.

Another Shade: Out of pride, daring to be compared with other women.

Another Shade: For your appalling proficiency.

Several Shades: For the way you ruffle our hair! — for the way you tell lies! — for the way you put your clothes back on!

Another Shade, *in a grave voice*: Women have Don Juan in the same way as men have whores!

Devil: Well, if it is enough for you, Prince Charming, at the point of death, to have been nothing but this base charmer, if that kind of glory pleases you ...

Don Juan: I loathe it!

Devil: What is left to you now?

Don Juan: What is left ... what is left ... Ah! I can feel that you are going to tear everything away from me, little by little!

Devil: Before roasting the Bluebird, I pluck him of his feathers!

Don Juan: What is left to me is my audacity. I don't care about anything ... even that I may have been taken for a questionable character. I know that I was always the first to break off our love affairs. You may have chosen me but it was I who left you!

The Shades:

He went this way

He'll come back that way!

Don Juan: He doesn't come back. I am the man who excels himself in continually tearing himself away from odious routine; the man who, always and only obeying his own instincts, bounds perilously over foolish moral concerns to fulfil his own great destiny! Don't you think that, ignoring all conventional boundaries, I've certainly run my life 'without rules, beyond the law' ...

Devil: I think you've been reading too much of what they write about you! ...

Don Juan: And I've used the time well to make progress these last ten years ...

Devil: A progress which was nothing but a flight!

Don Juan: Me, afraid?

Devil: Yes, afraid to stop running!

Don Juan: Afraid?

Devil: Of falling in love one day! The hero of love was fleeing from love!

Don Juan: Afraid?

Devil: Of being the first at the rendez-vous.

A Shade: Of having to wait.

Don Juan: Me, so carefree and joyful!

Another Shade: Who was afraid of showing tenderness!

Don Juan: Me, who made love with a song!

Another Shade: Like one whistling in the dark!

Another Shade, *speaking louder and louder:* You fled from woman to woman, like a man fleeing from tree to tree trying to avoid a skilful archer.

Another Shade, *in a high-pitched voice*: He used each new woman's body he encountered to make a rampart against some former lover!

Another Shade: He was afraid!

All the Shades, *crying out*: He was afraid!

Another Shade, *solemnly*: Of suffering!

Another Shade: Afraid of the sharp knife of pain to sculpt his soul that man virtually has the right to insist on from a woman!

Another Shade: Coward, who bore beneath a defrauded heaven the shame of an unblemished brow!

All the Shades: Coward!

Don Juan, *shaking his fist at the Shades:* Yes, you are insulting me, you crazed vindictive creatures, because you were never able to be the first to run away!

Devil, *laying a heavy hand on Don Juan's shoulder:* So that's what being a superhuman consists of, is it? Being the first to run away?

Don Juan: *straightening up*: No.

Devil: What have you been, then?

Don Juan: Oh!

Devil, *shaking him as he laughs in triumph*: Which way are you going to twist and turn now, to discover a destiny where there was only disorder? Search! Is there nothing left to you?

Don Juan, *trying to stand up straight*: There is ...

Devil, *sardonically*: Still fighting then?

Don Juan, *upright again, despairingly*: Still fighting!

Devil, *coldly:* In Greek it's called *Agonia*. Your final fight, your death throes.

Don Juan, *drawing himself up to his full height*: My death agony seizes on a new pride.

Devil, *smiling*: You change sticks as often as Punch!

Don Juan: There is this, that I was always, ferociously, the man who takes the woman away from another man: the lover! I never paled when another man's name was mentioned!

Devil: To make you pale now it is enough to mention ...

Don Juan: Who?

Half of the Shades: Romeo!

The Other Half: Tristan!

Don Juan: Ah! Be quiet!

The Shades on the right: Tristan!

The Shades on the left: Romeo!

A Shade: They were the true lovers. You took advantage of the longings they inspired in our souls. All you did was finish off the wounded, you plunderer!

Don Juan: It's not true! My name lives on in your memories ...

A Shade: In our memories of embraces but not of our sighs!

Don Juan: Oh!

The Shades: Romeo! — Tristan!

A Shade: Even when we lay in your arms, they were still our gods, for we were blaspheming against them!

The Shades: Romeo!

A Shade: Go and pursue your immortal rival!

The Shades: Tristan!

A Shade: You can't kill them in a duel!

Don Juan: Will you be quiet?

A Shade: Their fame disturbs you! You may have had all women, but you've not truly possessed a single one.

Don Juan: But at least — and you can't take this way from me — I have made women suffer ...

Devil: But you didn't understand their suffering!

Don Juan: Pah! What does that matter? I ravaged their tearful faces as Attila did the countryside, without trying to understand them. I remain the scourge of the most powerful of the gods! That's more than Tristan was! Or Romeo! That's what love is: one person suffers while the other one looks on. And I was always the other one, and that is what I hold onto. My eyes were cold as I watched them weep.

Devil: What it is to have travelled in England!

Don Juan: I know my own power.

Devil: Find out how great it really is.

Don Juan: What do you mean?

Devil, *taking a goblet from the table and handing it to Don Juan:* Take this fragile cup. This evening each love phantom carries like a jewel, in the corner of her mask, the largest tear she ever shed, in crystallised form. Collect them in this cup and we will hear them ...

Don Juan, *going round with the cup*: Thank you.

Devil: ... drop with a tinkle, like an offering.

Don Juan: For the soul of Don Juan! May the Devil repay you! Thank you!

Devil: To cut this short ...

Don Juan: Thank you very much!

Devil: ... Tears! All fall at once into this cup!

Don Juan: Thank you! — The cup is full! How it sparkles! Moon, my old colleague, come and make my fortune shine like silver! It was I who drew all these tears from women!

Speaking to the tears: Did you suffer, then? Did you suffer?

To the Devil: These tears will keep me cool in hell! All these trickled down cheeks because of me!

Devil: You are betting on these now, then?

Don Juan: I am winning with them, Demon! After all, for someone in your line, a goblet of tears is like a stoup of holy water.

Devil: It's true that a tear will burn the Devil.

He fumbles in the pockets of his greatcoat.

But I have here ...

He draws out an enormous magnifying glass set in black steel.

Don Juan: What is that?

Devil: My lens. It's my weapon.

He starts to lay out the tears on the table.

We will put on this side the true tears, pure and without flaws. And on the other, the false ones.

Don Juan, *with a start*: What do you mean, the false ones?

Devil, *pushing the tears aside with his magnifying glass*: False. False. False. False.

Don Juan: And that one?

Devil: That's a tear shed by someone whom you would have found laughing with her maid if you'd returned unexpectedly.

Don Juan: This big one?

Devil: Was shed on account of a spoiled hat. It was only on second thoughts that it was redirected to you.

Don Juan: What about these two very long ones?

Devil: Pah!

Don Juan: That's what you say.

He snatches up a tear suddenly.

Ah! What kind are the clearest?

Devil: The secret ones!

Don Juan: Look, I've got a secret one here!

Devil: But I can touch it without being hurt. It's a tear someone pretended to hide from you. How is it that I can safely touch all these tears, even those due to a suffering soul?

A Shade: It's because they were part of the package.

Don Juan: What?

The Shade: When you take on Don Juan, my dear, it is to offer yourself the luxury of discovering how much he can make you suffer!

Another Shade: And how our tears will taste on his lips!

Another Shade: It's not surprising that the Devil can touch with impunity tears where pleasure is part of their value.

Another Shade: Tears that we wanted a cruel man to make us weep, are tears ...

Don Juan: That one devours!

A Shade: That one savours.

Devil: Even back in the time of Caesar Augustus, Ovid knew all about that!

Another Shade: They were part of the package, along with the flowers and the chocolates ...

Devil: Tears that give pleasure are not true tears! — Well, do you still have any tinsel sceptres left? Search!

Don Juan: That cry you keep repeating, that digs into me so, teaches me what my greatness really consists of: I was a seeker! I was the man who believed in hidden treasure, in a blue flower on a mountain-top ...

Devil: What it is to have travelled in Germany!

Don Juan: If you find it, that's because you never had a dream in the first place.

Devil: So your claim to greatness is that you never found your ideal?

Don Juan: Yes.

Devil: Ouch!

Don Juan: What is it?

Devil: When I put my hand on the table just then, I burnt myself ...

Don Juan: Oh!

Devil: This one is genuine!

Don Juan: What do you mean?

Devil: Now that is a tear!

Don Juan: Yes, its white light has even splashed over you.

Devil: Come and look at it!

They both bend over the tear.

What a subject for Rembrandt! The profiles of two damned creatures bent over a star!

Don Juan: Could a woman have let this fall? ...

A Voice, that of the White Shade: Yes.

Don Juan: Bah!

A Shade whiter and more silvered than the others glides forward.

White Shade: A woman who like a tear herself, fell!

Don Juan: Like a tear?

White Shade: A tear of pity.

Don Juan: For your blemished virtue?

White Shade: No, for your anguish.

Don Juan: Ah?

White Shade: For you are nothing but anguish! Anguish which in spite of the pride you throw up in defiance, needs the comfort of arms around it!

Don Juan: Who are you, then, you who mark your lost virtue with a shining star?

White Shade: I am she who says what she is aloud.

Don Juan: Your mind?

White Shade: It is my heart.

Don Juan: Your soul?

White Shade: It is my heart.

Don Juan: Your senses?

White Shade: They were my heart!

Don Juan: What is your name, White Shade?

White Shade: I am she who says her name, but quietly.

She murmurs a name in Don Juan's ear.

Don Juan: I don't remember this charming name.

White Shade: I am she who takes off her mask without affectation.

She takes off her mask.

Don Juan: I do not recognise this delightful face. You gave yourself to me?

White Shade: When you desired me.

Don Juan, *searching his memory, hand on brow:* What day was that? In what country were we?

His hand automatically goes to his waistcoat.

My list! It's been torn up!

Devil, *smiling:* Fortunately I have a copy!

From one of his pockets he swiftly pulls out a strange kind of wallet, from which his long fingers draw another list, which he presents with a graceful gesture to Don Juan.

Don Juan, *seizing the list:* Give it to me!

He starts searching through the list.

No? No? ... I have met her ... She does exist .... where is her name?

DEVIL: Search!

Don Juan, *with mounting agitation*: Her name ... her name ... her name ...Oh, how sad! It's the only name I didn't write on the list!

Devil: You only forgot one ...

Don Juan, *to the White Shade*: And it was you!

White Shade: That's life!

Devil: Now, you seeker who found your treasure without realising it, have I got you beaten?

Don Juan: I wrote down with great care the names of even the most foolish women, and ... But when all the names turned into gondolas, what brought you safely here across the water?

White Shade: There was a white space on the torn-up list!

Don Juan, *drawing himself up again suddenly*: But I've only lost the Ideal Woman once, out of a thousand and four women. Is that enough to bring me down?

White Shade, *who has mingled with the Shades on the left*: Only once?

Don Juan: She has fled.

White Shade, *passing to the right*: Only once?

Don Juan: Her voice is growing distant? ... Where are you? ... Why are you doing this?

White Shade: Only once?

Don Juan: Why are you making me pursue your voice from woman to woman, as if I'm following the sound of wings from tree to tree?

White Shade: To teach you ...

Don Juan: But where are you?

White Shade, *reappearing*: ... that you might have found me in each one of them, with a little love!

Don Juan, *seizing her*: You only existed in one woman!

White Shade: But I was waiting in all of them! You spent your life passing us by. Our hearts only beat when you listen to them, and you slept on our hearts without listening to them. You might have made each one of us bloom into the best of all companions, perhaps, if only you had tried ....

Other Shades: Me too! — Me too! — Me too!

White Shade: The chance was always there ...

Don Juan: Oh no!

White Shade: Yes, alas!

All the Shades: Yes, Don Juan!

Don Juan: An immense sob, drowning their bitterness, makes them stretch out their arms into infinity!

The Shades: Each one of us! — Each one of us! – Don Johnny! — Don Johann! — Don Juan! — Don Giovanni!

Devil: What? Let this flood of tenderness seize back their souls from me? Rise up, you bitches! Go back to hating him!

He moves downstage.

How easily eternal Man and eternal Woman would forget their differences if I wasn't there!

Don Juan, *to the White Shade*: I would have wanted to love you!

Devil: Die, knowing that she exists!

White Shade: No! As long as a flame continues to burn in my tear, Don Juan can try to find that he does have a heart.

Devil: Search! ... And if he is capable of truly loving a woman, I am vanquished!

White Shade: Love, even for a moment, the shade of she who was your mistress once! Take my head in your hands, like this, and say: 'I want to stroke ... I want to stroke ... I am stroking all the fair tresses I have ever dreamt of on this one chosen brow!'

Don Juan: I want to ....

Devil: Too late! For too long you were the enemy ...

White Shade: Say: ' I offer myself to love ...' Hold me close ...

Don Juan: I am holding you closely, and I give myself up to love ...

Devil: Like a wrestler who parries automatically in spite of himself when he is seeking to die!

Don Juan: No! I carry you off at last on my heart full of joy, your faithful lover!

All the Shades, *taking off their masks*: Faithful?

Don Juan: Oh! The silken masks have fallen! I can see their faces!

White Shade: All those faces which you know have lied to you?

Don Juan:I know that they have all lied to me, all lied ... But oh!

The Shades: Faithful?

Don Juan: If they have all lied to me, then they are all new women! No, I no longer have a heart for just one woman, as long as a new face is there to intrigue me ...

The Shades: Ha ha!

Don Juan, *to the White Shade*: Go away!

To the others: But don't exult, I am still invincible!

Devil: So, you were searching in order not to find what you sought?

Don Juan: It's possible! For if I had found it, I would have died of boredom. Don Juan was only interested in the search and in himself! For me, woman was just a pretext. No, don't exult! I possessed you as one who might take a sword, a goblet, Dionysius's flowering staff or a flaming torch, so that I could leap beyond myself all the better!

A Shade: Is this the latest source of pride you are putting on now, like a new suit of clothes?

Don Juan: Yes, all of you have only been the means by which I exalted myself!

Another Shade: That may well be true, Don Juan. So what you have done with this exaltation?

Don Juan: But ...

Another Shade: If you obtained from us all that you say you have, then, Don Juan ...

Another Shade: Then, Don Juan, give us your accounts! What did you do with that evening when, suffocating with pride, you stepped out of my gondola?

Another Shade: What have you done with those nights when I induced in you that lucid fever which should inspire great exploits?

All the Shades: Give us your accounts!

A Shade: If it is true that thanks to me you were able to leap above yourself, where did you leap to? What have you done that was immortal with even one second of my love?

Another Shade: Inspired by the beauty of my eyes, where is your work of art that rivals the Mona Lisa?

Don Juan: Be quiet!

Devil: At last, the sound of a genuine cry!

Another Shade: And the rose you used to pick from my hedge every morning as you left me, where is the poem in which it blooms again?

Don Juan: Ah! You have touched my most secret wound!

Another Shade: When, ready to give myself to you, I whispered 'Wherever you like!', what banners did you seize, to wrap me in for sheets?

Don Juan: Silence!

A Shade: And our exquisite time together in Sicily, what great? beautiful? demanding? work of art did it produce?

Devil: That's right, stab your long daggers of regret into this heart that turned aside from ambition into desire!

A Shade: Women have loved you. What have you done with that wonderful inner garden that blooms when someone knows they are loved? You are like Boabdil, turning his back on the Alhambra.

Another Shade: Seeing you emerge so frequently from our embraces, other men have hated you ... What have you done with their hatred?

Another Shade: What have you done with my kiss, the kiss of a queen? You should have felt obliged to become a king.

Another Shade: As for me, I was an actress. What you done with the sighs you breathed through Electra's veils?

All the Shades: Don Juan! Don Juan!

Don Juan: What is this wild clamour? A riot of phantoms?

The Shades: If we really were all these things for you ...

Devil: Stab the futile Caesar!

The Shades: What have you done with them? The flowering staff? — the flaming torch? — the goblet? — the sword?

White Shade: Don Juan ...

Don Juan: Even you ?

White Shade: What have you done with my tear?

Don Juan: Yes, you were quite right to shed a tear over my anguish. Hearts do not always realise what regrets they may have later. After all my opportunities to be great, strong or sad, all I have done is to make a list ...

Devil: He should get down on his knees on his list!

The Shades: On your knees! On your knees! Yes, he deserves to stay on his knees, because, only wanting us and nothing beyond us, he made of each of us the Woman who never leads to anything but another Woman!

Don Juan: I feel cold!

A Shade: Because he made of love — the love he discredits — just one brief moment of pleasure, leading only to other such moments!

Don Juan: I do not repent ... Oh, what pains are these? They call someone 'Don Juan' to mean he is victorious, but every man has his day! A day when he fulfils his potential, when he says to himself: 'I am!' But I haven't had my day!

Devil: You've only had their nights!

Don Juan: Ah! Don't think I repent in the least ... but Don Juan, that name recalls Don Juan of Austria, victor of the battle of Lepanto, not me! Why is it that, at the point of death, one wants to remember some deed which links you with the future? I do not repent ... What strange fires are these that I feel? ... Death, do you love life so much that you avenge it? So must the fallen runner die, burnt by the torch he failed to pass on?

Devil: So now, do you still believe the worm is in all the fruits of the Tree?

Don Juan: Ah! If one's will can carve fruit from marble, if by creating something beautiful, I see now that one can vanquish the worm in the fruit and the worm in the tomb! ...

Devil: As you suffer the agonies of dying, does it satisfy you to have lived, like Venice, on your own reflection?

Don Juan: No! At the moment of death, one must have created something. You cannot know what I am suffering.

Devil: He he!

Don Juan: Oh! To think that nothing living will come of my having lived! Do you know it, this suffering?

Devil: It's my own suffering. That's what hell is. No one who has created anything is down there.

Don Juan: Do you pity me?

Devil: I understand you. I am not capable of pity.

Wanting to drag Don Juan away: Come on, let's go! You're one of those people of whom nothing remains, not a word, not a gesture!

Don Juan: Ah yes! There is! A word! A gesture! That famous word and gesture by which I announced the revolution to come! Do you remember that one day, when I was escaping from the authorities in the depths of the countryside with my cloak thrown across my face, I came across the Poor Man ...

Devil: All right, let's talk about that for a bit.

Don Juan: He was asking for alms, for the love of his God. As I gave him a golden guinea, I uttered these words, which made the coin blaze: 'For the love of humanity'!

Devil: Humanity!

Don Juan: I was the first in history to throw out that word!

Devil: What it is to have travelled through France!

Don Juan: Loosen your grip! This time my destiny is clear. I think the future will owe me something after all. It was I who, meeting the Poor Man at the edge of a wood, freed him from his resignation to his lot.

Out of the way, Devil! It is from libertines that Liberty with a capital 'l' gets its boldness! I have not lived in vain after all. I can find him again, that Poor Man!

Devil:: Dare to speak to him, then!

Scene Two

DON JUAN, THE DEVIL, THE THOUSAND AND THREE SHADES, THE WHITE SHADE, THE POOR MAN

Don Juan: My piece of gold still shines in his hand, which he seems to be holding out to me ... Phantom, what do you want with me?

Poor Man: This, first: to give it back to you!

He throws the coin at Don Juan's head.

Don Juan, *staggering, his forehead wounded*: Ah!

Devil: You deserved to perish from that gift!

Don Juan, *to the Poor Man, who is walking silently towards him, hands open*: But let me explain ... liberty ...

Poor Man, *raising his enormous hand*: Steady on! That's too big a subject for you to concern yourself with all of a sudden.

Don Juan: The People ...

Poor Man: No, Don Juan, your concerns don't go any higher than a skirt!

Don Juan: But the Future ...

Devil, *to the Poor Man*: Stuff these grand self-justifying claims of his down his throat! Are debauched fellows to end up as apostles?

Don Juan: But I did revolt!

Poor Man: Not on behalf of others!

Don Juan: You're not going to ...

Poor Man: I am going to strangle you for having defiled those words we use to express our hopes!

Don Juan: So, a second Commander rolls up his sleeves?

Poor Man: The first Commander's hands were too white to kill the hero of those who do nothing!

Don Juan: But listen! I can be useful to you, man of the people! I can ...

White Shade: Oh, as long as there is a flame in that tear, Don Juan can try to find a soul for himself ...

Devil: He'll have to be quick, then! It's about to go out!

Don Juan: I am bold ...

Poor Man, *sniggering*: Oh yes?

Don Juan: Cunning ...

Poor Man: Yes?

Don Juan: I have what it takes to be a leader ...

Poor Man: Yes?

Don Juan: I like destroying things ...

Poor Man: Yes?

Don Juan: And, if it comes to bloodshed ...

Poor Man, *suddenly serious and terrible:* Yes, it may be necessary!

Don Juan: I can commit ...

All the Shades, *throwing off their cloaks*: A crime?

Don Juan: Ah! Their silken mantles have dropped to the ground! ... What was I saying?

Devil: Search!

Don Juan: Oh, you're stopping me! I can't think!

Poor Man: You were talking of committing ...?

The Shades: A crime?

Don Juan: Ah no — only sins! It's too late now, I can no longer think of serving a worthy cause, not while their shoulders are white and their bosoms rosy. Kill me!

Devil: Nothing grows where the goat has grazed. That's the bottom line. All the rest was added on later. Now I shall press my horny hoof onto your pale forehead.

Don Juan: Ah! Pity the poor male! Why must one always betray everything just for that? Men who could seek other aims. And yet, there is more to life worth seeking! Oh, why is it enough for human flesh that a wisp of veil around the mystery can usurp the place of the mystery itself! How is it that a great heart which could nourish a great vulture becomes a snack for Lesbia's sparrow! Kill me! Or I shall be again be at the mercy of my morbid obsession, grovelling to these Shades for a thrill, coming back to them like a dog to its ...

Devil: So have I now stripped off your final skin? This is what it comes to: your intelligence! ...

Don Juan: Ah!

Devil: ... Your strength!

Don Juan: Ah!

Devil: ... Your will-power!

Don Juan: Ah!

Devil: ... Your liberty! Do you remember the word used by Punch?

Don Juan: Be quiet!

Voice of Punch, *offstage*: Debauchery!

Don Juan: So this is my reward for thinking myself to be in the vanguard of human insolence: that Punch should have the last word!

White Shade: But there was more to it than that. He's hiding his ultimate excuse out of pride ...

Don Juan: No excuses!

White Shade: He was never able to come to terms with himself: those who do not love themselves need others to love them.

Don Juan: No excuses! At least I am dying with my fists clenched, without having begged for death! Take me to hell! I'm yearning for it!

Devil, *to the Poor Man*: Drag over to me that fine empty costume into which everyone will slide his dream ...

Don Juan: What's this?

Devil: You'll soon see what an amusing little hell you're going to have!

Don Juan: The hell of monsters ... Nero, Caligula?

Devil: No, a little hell of cloth that gets trundled about.

Don Juan: What, the puppet show? I want to be a damned soul!

Devil: You will be a puppet, and you will play the adulterer over and over again on that tiny stage, for all eternity.

Don Juan: Mercy! The eternal fires!

Devil: No, the eternal theatre.

Don Juan: I don't want to ...

Devil, *to the Poor Man*: Come and strangle him for me without further ado!

Don Juan, *struggling in the arms of the Poor Man*: ... be a puppet! ... I don't want to ...

Devil: Come and surrender yourself to the hands of the puppet master!

Don Juan: ... be a puppet!

Devil: The show's about to start! The bell is ringing! Come and sit down on the ground, all you women!

Poor Man: Come on!

Don Juan: I don't want to be a puppet!

Devil, *to the Poor Man*: Drag him over here!

Don Juan: No, not into that little booth! Into the great circle of fire that my pride has merited!

Poor Man: Let's go!

Don Juan: I want to suffer! I've never suffered! I've earned my hell! I've got a right to my hell!

Devil: Hell is where I choose to place it. I'm the one who decides. Certain famous men endure hell as their statues. You're going to spend it as a puppet!

Don Juan: At least I shall be defying you! Marble is dead but a puppet is alive! And after all, in this guise I shall have to ...

Devil: Shine?

Don Juan: Yes, I shall make them laugh again ...

Devil: Who are you talking about?

Don Juan: The young girls! I shall be amusing them under the eyes of their parents!

White Shade: Oh, you who could have fulfilled the greatest destinies!

Don Juan: I shall sing, as I beat the dolls with my stick ...

White Shade: You who could have wielded the mightiest swords!

Don Juan: I shall sing: 'I am ...'

White Shade: Oh! The flame in my tear has gone out!

Don Juan: 'I am the famous Burla ...'

Poor Man, *pushing Don Juan into the puppet booth*: That's enough!

Devil: Now, Don Juan, you who would recreate yourself in my image, become a puppet!

Don Juan, *appearing in the puppet booth as a puppet*:

' The famous Burlador! ... Burlador ...'

White Shade, *with infinite despair*: What a pity!

CURTAIN